The Cooking of Music
and
Other Essays

The Cooking of Music
and
Other Essays

SHEILA DHAR

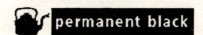

Published by
PERMANENT BLACK
D-28 Oxford Apartments, 11 I.P. Extension,
New Delhi 110092

Distributed by
ORIENT LONGMAN LTD.
Bangalore Bhopal Bhubaneshwar Chandigarh
Chennai Ernakulam Guwahati Hyderabad Jaipur
Kolkata Lucknow Mumbai New Delhi Patna

Copyright © SHEILA DHAR 2001
ISBN 81-7824-028-9
First published 2001

Typeset in Bembo by Eleven Arts
Printed by Pauls Press, Delhi 110020
Binding by Saku Binders, Khanpur, New Delhi

Publisher's Note

Sheila Dhar died on 26 July 2001, soon after finalising the typescript of this book. Some of the essays are new versions of earlier ones and will sound familiar to those who know her work. The majority, however, were written for this volume, after some careful cannibalisations from the author's own earlier writings.

Partho Datta refused to let us put his name on the cover as 'Editor', but that is what he has been.

The Afterword provides biographical information on Sheila Dhar, and appreciation of her artistic skills.

Contents

1. Sound and Hindustani Music — 9
2. The Raga: An Inward Journey — 13
3. Reflections on the Kirana Legacy — 21
4. The Cooking of Music — 37
5. Fear of Recording: The Non-Westernness of Hindustani Music — 43
6. Sunlight in the Raga — 52
7. Begum Akhtar — 61
8. Go, Lady, Go: Lady Linlithgow and the Taming of Raga Adana — 70
9. A Taste of British Guiana — 76
10. The Many-Splendoured Harmonium — 84
11. The New Face of Listening — 91
    Afterword: Two Obituaries of Sheila Dhar — 107

ONE

Sound and Hindustani Music

Reverence for sound is basic to Indian philosophy. Some schools, specially the Yoga and the Tantra, equate *Nada Brahman*, the primordial sound with the Absolute, the Creator, the cause of the phenomenal world. While Nada is the sound of the Universe, the subtlest of all elements, Brahman is existence, blissful awareness, the taintless, imperishable supreme deity. It is significant that *shakti*, the energy of the creative power of Brahman, is also called *nada* (sound) or *sabda* (word). In the Hindu scheme of things, sound is of two kinds. The first, *anahata nada*, or unstruck sound, is not a matter of sense perception but a mystic experience in which sound and light are fused together in a direct perception of the Absolute. It is the very hum of creation. The second, which concerns us here, is *ahata nada*, or created sound, which in its very distinction from the first implies an awareness of it.

The origins of the music of India are thus deeply spiritual and devotional. Symbolically, most gods and goddesses of the pantheon are associated with music and rhythm. The creative energy of Brahma is deified as Saraswati who is inseparable from the *vina* or lute, Siva dances to the beat of the *damaru* drums, and Krishna enchants his devotees with the strains of the bamboo flute. All manifestations of godhood are traditionally propitiated with song and dance. The beginnings of Indian music can be traced back to the chanting of the Sama Veda nearly four thousand years ago. The primacy of the voice and the association of musical sound with prayer were established early in the history of Indian music and remain essentially unchanged.

Music has been a cultivated art in India for at least three thousand years. Classical music today is a direct descendant of the ancient tradition, preserved, elaborated, and developed by hereditary musicians through the ages and passed on orally from master to disciple. This music is as true and real a part of life as it ever was, bringing to the present generation the still vibrant awareness of times long past and a range of emotional experiences that the modern world cannot provide.

The ancient music of India had been nourished from the earliest times by diverse streams including the religious, the folk, the tribal, and the courtly. An example of the first is the *prabandha*, a poetic arrangement sung in a preset melody to a fixed rhythmic cycle. The outstanding Sanskrit opera, *Gita Govinda*, by the twelfth-century poet Jayadeva, was composed in this style and became a landmark in the history of Indian music. The theme of Jayadeva's work was the divine love of Radha and Krishna. The exceptional literary and musical merit of Jayadeva's work continued to inspire followers and imitators of the devotional genre for nearly four hundred years after him. The prabandha no longer forms a part of the repertoire of classical musicians today, and the original music of *Gita Govinda* is lost to us. However, the lilting lines of Jayadeva are still sung to tunes set locally in various parts of India, and improvised upon by dancers.

Around the twelfth century the northern part of the country began to receive a fresh infusion—melodic and Sufic influences from Persia. The contributions of Amir Khusrau, a poet and musician at the court of the Pathan ruler Alauddin Khilji, had a decisive hand in giving a new orientation to music. After the thirteenth century the music of India branched into two systems—the Hindustani or northern which is discussed here, and the Karnatak or southern. Although both follow the same basic principles, they differ sharply in musical intention and ethos.

The prabandha mentioned earlier was the precursor of the *dhruvapada* or *dhrupad* which reached its full flowering in north India in the fifteenth and sixteenth centuries. This was an age of revival and exuberance, and under the patronage of enlightened rulers like Raja Man Singh Tomar of Gwalior and the Mughal emperor Akbar the dhrupad form flourished and reached its peak.

The dhrupad is a stately, formal, closely structured composition in which the text, usually in the Braja dialect of Hindi, consists mainly of hymns of praise in honour of gods and goddesses, and of heroes. Dhrupad singing always starts with *alaap* or free elaboration of the raga or melody in slow, medium, and fast tempos. The syllables used in this part, which precedes the text, are said to be taken from the various names of God and the atmosphere sought to be created is one of selfless devotion and serenity. The text of the composition follows in rhythm cycles of great grandeur and gravity which are articulated by a two-headed drum. The melodic movement uses pure notes and broad glissandos. No embellishments or tonal graces are allowed to interfere with the clear enunciation of the words. A dhrupad performance is a vigorous act of devotion to both the subject of the hymn and to the raga or melody in which it is rendered. This form survives to this day and is highly treasured by the connoisseur. A variation within this genre is the *dhamar* which is somewhat less austere in intent since it usually describes the youthful Krishna and his playful amours during Holi. The dhrupad and dhamar are a continuation of ancient classical textual forms enriched and modified by contemporary folk traditions and as such are the precursors of all later musical models.

A parallel development with the dhrupad and one which gave another powerful impetus to music in north India was the revival of the *bhakti* cult under Chaitanya in the later part of the fifteenth century. For nearly two hundred years there was a great upsurge of devotional music that spread to all parts of the country. The large number of saint-composers who wrote and sang simple, moving songs of extraordinary beauty during this period did much to make the world of music accessible to all, and to attune the Indian ear to receive the sophistication and refinement of later musical developments.

The most widely practiced classical form of the Hindustani system today is the *khayal*, a Persian term loosely meaning 'idea' or 'flight of the imagination'. The khayal had first appeared soon after dhrupad, but came into its own in the early decades of the eighteenth century. As the designation of this form suggests, it allows the personality of the musician greater scope for expression and personal feeling than the dhrupad. It represents in many ways a subtle shift in musical values. The ideal of the structured awe-inspiring ritual of devotion seems to make room for the individual musician's aspiration. The presentation of a khayal is not the rendering of a song, for here it is not the words that are set to music but almost a reverse process.

This is not the case in *thumri*, a light classical manifestation which was developed in the middle of the nineteenth century by Wajid Ali Shah, the Nawab of Awadh. In this genre the stress is on the text of the lyric, which always has a romantic theme of love and longing, in the poetic folk language of the region where Krishna is believed to have spent his childhood and youth. Thumri singing is the art of conveying the meaning of the words through acute suggestion. A skilful performer can give the same line of a lyric a hundred clearly different meanings through musical manipulation alone.

Although thumri is based on classical ragas, it is far less demanding in the matter of purity. Tradition allows the performer almost unlimited freedom to indulge himself. He may not only mix ragas but also insert textual material such as couplets in Urdu, Hindi or Brajbhasha to make his rendering more poignant and instantly appealing. Current forms such as *dadra, bhajan, kajri, chaiti, jhoola* and even *ghazal* are other manifestations in the same genre which accommodate a spontaneity unthinkable in dhrupad or khayal.

TWO

The Raga: An Inward Journey

The preoccupation of the traditional Hindustani musician is predominantly spiritual in the sense that he must first find and activate the inner source, the centre of his being, the *bindu* or core within himself where he rings most true and then draw it out with his life-breath, *prana*, and proffer it as sound. Tradition exhorts the musician to plumb the depths within him rather than seek range and variety. The *shadaja*, the tonic note, is the musical bindu which symbolises eternal being. The term shadaja literally means 'born of the six (notes).' It is the key which admits the listening ear to the meaning of the music. The tanpura or stringed drone which invariably accompanies Indian music continuously offers the reposeful sound of the shadaja. The musical utterance, whether vocal or instrumental, is the unbroken melodic line. These melodic lines are seen as an extension of the shadaja and draw their being and energy from it. The music unfolds when the reposeful but dominant tonic nucleus of the shadaja becomes charged through concentration and intensity and begins to emit musical rays, so to speak. These melodic rays and lines strain away from the shadaja and return to rest in it, thus creating pulsating patterns of tension and release.

Hindustani musicians undergo rigorous training and possess incredible skill and control. However, the central object of their labours is not the cultivation of a 'beautiful' tone but the development of an almost limitless capability in articulation. The physical sound of the music is, in ideal circumstances, only a medium and not the end product. To the connoisseur, a voice is only as beautiful as what it conveys. The physical body of the music is to the musician what a writing tool is to the poet. The listener is trained to tune in to the highly-charged state of consciousness of the performer rather than to the physical condition of the sound that carries the music. Consequently, Indian ears are somewhat indifferent to the outer perfection of musical sound. Some of the most revered musicians have been and are people in their seventies. Their glory is in the truth of their experience and though their voices might have lost superficial lustre, the purity of their intention still shines through and is always the focus of attention for the initiated listener.

The human voice is considered the supreme instrument and the major musical tradition is embodied in a great variety of vocal styles and forms. Most stringed and wind instruments recall some quality or aspect of the voice. The singing voice in Indian music is the earthy unbeautified voice of everyday speech, not a musical escape from it.

Raga is a central concept in all Indian music. It is a Sanskrit term which literally means passion, colour and attachment, something that has 'the effect of colouring the hearts of men.' There is an implied value here of an intensity, a singleness of colour—not a rainbow—that the performer must create anew in order to suffuse 'the hearts of men'. Most of the ragas which inhabit the world of musicians today are highly developed and schematic versions of the primitive melodies of the various tribal and folk cultures of the country. Each raga is an incipient melodic idea which uses at least five tones of the octave. Each has strict rules of ascent and descent, prescribed resting places, characteristic phrases and a distinct ethos of its own. Each is assigned to a particular time of day or season and is invested with the power to evoke a state of feeling related to both the human condition and to nature. There are pre-dawn ragas like Lalit which are associated with the meeting of darkness and light. All major morning ragas such as Bhairav and Todi are sombre and devotional, for morning is a time for prayer and meditation. As the light gets stronger, more luminous ragas such as Jaunpuri and Bilawal enter the field. The Sarang family of ragas, performed in the early afternoon, are full of sunlight and emit a 'shimmering, leafy green colour'. The late afternoon ragas, like Multani and Patdeep, are restless, intense with heat, and seem to speak of a time when the day's activity is at its peak. As the sun sets, the sedate and tranquil evening ragas take over. Most members of the Kalyan family of ragas belong to this time of calm introspection and radiate a deep serenity. Between sunset and late night there are lyrical and romantic ragas such as Des, Tilang, and Khamaj. Ragas that are performed deep into the night, for example, Darbari Kanhara and Malkaus, are profoundly searching creations, full of magic, mystery and depth. Additionally, there are ragas for the rainy season, for the spring-time, and for the harvest festival of Holi. Today, there are no more than a hundred ragas in the collective repertoire of the Hindustani musician. These are survivors from the thousands that were introduced at one stage or another through permissible choice and permutation of tones within the octave.

To the conditioned ear, each phrase of one of these ragas is like a limb that reveals the identity of the whole being and has the power to evoke in the listener its entire image. It is significant that the sequential order of tones in a melodic line does not mean anything by itself. Its expression and effect depend on its dynamics—on how it swerves towards or away from a tone or from silence; how it curves, dives, wafts, spirals, trails or plummets; on where it gathers its greatest weight and luminosity and on its grain and texture. Two entirely different ragas quite often have the same sequence of tones. It is the sculpting of the melodic line connecting the sequence that distinguishes one from the other, just as the usage of a word and the tone of voice in which it is spoken are what determine its exact meaning.

Hindustani music does not isolate individual notes of the scale but glides over the intervals that separate them. For this reason there is no exact universally accepted system of notation. For the same reason keyboard instruments are considered to be unsuitable. However, the melodic line does pass through tones, semi-tones, and quarter-tones, the frequencies of which are identified for purposes of clarity. There are twelve *svaras* or notes in the scale of Hindustani music, and ten *shrutis* or microtones. Literally shruti means any sound which is capable of being heard and theoretically there could be numberless shrutis in the octave, but only ten are used in Hindustani music. The word svara means 'that which is luminous in itself.' To qualify as svara a note must shine like a gem in its setting of microtones.

In Hindustani music, a note is not thought of as a fixed point but, rather, an area through which a melodic line passes. The more developed a musician's sensibility and concentration, the more extensive this area becomes. It is these 'areas' that the musician shapes with delicate nuances and elaborate graces in the course of his extempore exploration of the raga. Obviously this kind of music cannot be captured in its entirety in a written score. The way to enter the music is by attentively following the moving melodic line whose many subtle and dynamic forms etch detailed and intricate shapes which are of great musical interest.

The musical vocabulary of intervals is a shared heritage familiar even to the uninitiated. Each note in the scale when heard along with the tonic yields, as a word does in language, a colour and emotional charge. For instance, one might say arbitrarily that the perfect fifth is red, positive, strong; that the third is sky blue, tranquil, lucid; and that the flat third or sixth is grey, introspective, plaintive; and so on. This sense of the inherent emotional content of intervals is a common language understood in general terms by all who share the regional culture of which this system of music is a product, just as those who are not themselves painters might still react to an array of primary colours. The skilled musician uses these colours, leading his audience into delicately shaded areas, carrying them all through the creative process, line by line, stroke by stroke, colour by colour—until he has infused into them the portrait of the raga as he conceives of it at the time. Dhrupad,

THE RAGA: AN INWARD JOURNEY

khayal and thumri compositions are not really compositions in the Western sense and allow far greater latitude to the performer, especially the last. If the musician were to sing or play the same 'composition' several times, each would be an irreproducible original, though each would be based on the musical concept of the piece that is being rendered.

Each composition or *bandish* is set in a known *tala* or rhythmic arrangement of beats in a cyclic manner. Each rhythmic cycle is divided into sections which may or may not be equal. It is complete in itself and continues to repeat itself faithfully throughout the performance of a particular piece. As the melodic lines strain away from the shadaja and return to it, so the beats of a tala emanate from the *sam,* the first beat of the cycle which carries the greatest emphasis, and travel in a descending arc to the *khali* (empty), at which point the rhythm gathers momentum again to ascend and culminate in the sam. The tala sets up an elaborate pulsating rhythmic pattern which the musician uses as a sort of frame on which to weave his melodic threads. The sam is both the beginning and the end of the cycle, and commands special attention, as the drum stroke here coincides with a melodic climax in the composition, creating each time a burst of musical energy, a sense of arriving. This repetitive musical travelling and arriving generates a pattern of tension and release which is a special characteristic of Hindustani music.

In an actual performance, the singer first 'awakens' the shadaja, then in wordless syllables and in free rhythm draws some evocative melodic lines to usher in the raga in which the piece is set. This is the crucial *alaap* part, the foundation on which everything else will rest. He then begins the composition, guiding the drummer as to the intended tempo and indicating where he must come in with the first stroke or sam of the tala. After the first cue, the tabla player needs no further direction, only the most sensitive listening so that the beat is in sympathy with the musical intention and provides an unobtrusive setting.

After the bandish has been outlined, the performer develops the raga in the manner of a pyramid, often using the suggestions implicit in the composition as a model for the proliferating lines. He explores and cultivates the lower regions of the scale in great depth in slow tempo and then rises in the scale of the raga, gradually increasing the tempo. The nature of this expression, which develops vertically as it were, is an intensification, a gradual accumulation of meaning, rather than an extended statement. However, it still demands to be heard as a totality, for a part of it would be as meaningless as a truncated sentence. The first sounding of the upper tonic, the *taar shadaja*, is a climactic moment, for only at this point is the delineation of the raga completed.

The music is not 'prepared' beforehand and rigidly presented but is a live communication in which the listener contributes to the reality of each moment. The ideal of the singer is to share with the listener all phases of the creative process, much like an idea developed in extempore speech. The natural form of performance of this music is therefore the live chamber concert. The portrait of the raga, presented by the musician, is in a sense the product of the attention of all those present at its unfolding. This situation is quite different from that of the Western composer whose work is undertaken in relative isolation.

The musician envisions a heightened state of being through the portraiture of the lines of the raga. The lines, colours, and feelings offered by the raga create a field of awareness in which the listener can share in the intended evocation. What the listeners hear and acknowledge is the validation of what the singer is discovering in the moment. This live chemistry of participation is a vital factor in traditional performances where the performer is the leader and the listener the follower. Ideally, both experience the full portrait in sound simultaneously.

Of course, music can and is presented at many levels. There is a greater demand for and therefore greater abundance of musical products with ready appeal. What makes such music unacceptable to the connoisseur is not its elementary character—for the greatest music can be extremely simple—but the fact that the musician is not seriously involved with a vision and is only making a studied effort to simulate it. What is significant here is that even in this simulation he acknowledges the essentially spiritual character of classical music by taking the trouble to imitate it.

As there can be many styles of calligraphy so there are a number of styles in which the melodic line can be drawn on the canvas of silence. These styles of Hindustani classical music are called *gharanas*, and function like closed guilds. Gharana literally means 'family' in the sense of lineage. The personal style, musical attitudes, and predispositions of an acknowledged master are what give a gharana its distinctly recognisable melodic movement and dialect.

The transmission of traditional music from master to disciple is a very serious matter in India. *Seena ba seena*, from breast to breast, is a commonly used phrase in this context. What the *ustad* (master) passes on to the *shagird* (disciple) is the whole experience of his inner musical self, his entire 'quality'. Therefore nothing less than total commitment on the part of the pupil is acceptable. He has to be a vehicle that is fit to receive, cherish, and perpetuate the life and work of a great musical mind. The teaching is oral and very often secretive. The master teaches perhaps a son, or a nephew or son-in-law, or a deserving pupil who has proved himself trustworthy in every sense. For an 'outsider' to be accepted as a disciple is rare, an overwhelming and remarkable thing which happens only to the fortunate few. Reverence, humility, and the aspiration to merge with something bigger than oneself are such an integral part of the process that they almost enter the music as values, along with the values of purity and restraint. The highest compliment for an Indian musician is to be told that his work is reminiscent of the masters he admires and that he is a torch bearer. To most musicians this brings more satisfaction and fulfilment than being considered unique.

The characteristics of the dialect and style of each gharana originate in the personalities of the individuals who founded them. Even though the faithful preservation of these characteristics is applauded by purists today, with the greater access provided by electronic aids and increased physical mobility there is much more exchange and contact, acknowledged and unacknowledged, between the gharanas. Many examples of borrowing and mixing are audible on concert stages in India.

One of the remarkable things about traditional Hindustani music is the coexistence in its practice of the most rigorous discipline and a degree of freedom that is truly astonishing. The manifold disciplines are rigid and uncompromising: the rules of the raga, the time of the day, the intention of the composition, the confining frame of the tala, the prescribed form of presentation, faithfulness to the *vani* or style of utterance. These and many other considerations bind the musician, but at the same time tradition offers him extraordinary freedom to express his being. He is free to explore the areas in between the rigid 'notes' of the keyboard and free from objective time. The raga performance is an evocation that aspires to break free of time by itself becoming a kind of time, with a breath and movement of its own. The unfolding of a raga is an act of persuasion and the time it takes is a purely subjective matter for both the musician and the listener. It is the attention of the listener, mobilised by an abundance of shared conditions, which can help this experience come to life.

THREE

Reflections on the Kirana Legacy

When we speak of the *gharana* of a traditional musician, we mean the family traits of the music he practises and owes allegiance to. The concept of musical gharanas is physically comparable to that of families or clans in general, but in reality it is far more extensive and complicated. It signifies not only the physical characteristics, temperamental leanings and attitudes of the founder, in the same way as it would in the case of the ancestral line of a family, but much else that is contributed by all the talent that has come to drink at the fount of the master. This interaction and experience leaves an enduring imprint on the common pool of the gharana's wealth.

A musical gharana invariably grows around the genius of a creative master whose achievements automatically attract a collection of aspirants, admirers, and disciples. Traditionally, these masters command the kind of unqualified reverence that is associated with religious gurus. Their followers not only unquestioningly adhere to the musical principles laid down by them but also unconsciously imitate the physical characteristics of their role models. This small nucleus grows and widens as the style associated with the master gains prestige and acceptability among music lovers. Each gharana has a temperament since it reflects and carries within itself the seeds of the personality of the master with whom it originated. The outstanding *khayal* gharanas today are Gwalior, Agra, Kirana, Jaipur-Athrauli, and Patiala, each named after the original place of residence of the *ustad* or family of ustads around whom closely guarded musical guilds grew and flourished. It is fascinating to observe how the traits, aptitudes and predilections of a master mould the musical approach and attitudes of a gharana.

Practitioners of the Gwalior gharana, the oldest of all khayal gharanas, clearly show their respect for both the vigour and the rigour of older religious forms such as dhrupad and give precedence to the demands of the *bandish* over that of their personal musical urges. Their aim is to adhere strictly to the structure and frame of the composition they are presenting even while improvising freely and spontaneously. This can be quite a feat of musicianship. Both the rhythmic and melodic aspects share the musician's attention equally. In a sense, the *gayaki* of the Gwalior gharana is the most disciplined and demanding because the practising musician cannot afford the luxury of specialising in any one aspect which pleases him most. He must master all the facets of music and a great variety of techniques if he is to be faithful to the original style.

Most other gharanas on the other hand display far more freedom and discrimination in deciding which aspects of music they would like to stress and make their speciality. These preferences of course reflect the personal musical affiliations of the masters they follow. For instance the Agra gharana is known for bold, staccato movements and full-throated evocations in which rhythmic interplay is used to enhance the persuasiveness of the music. The ideal that all singers of this gharana try to imitate is the overt and robust style of emoting that was characteristic of Ustad Faiyyaz Khan, their idol.

The Kirana gharana traces delicate three-dimensional arcs, and draws from silence deeply searching spirals. The true Kirana musician believes that each *jagah* or 'place' in the scale of a raga is not a point but a musical area that must be explored anew each time and brought to life in the living moment. This introspective approach is also reflected in their style of raga development. The base of the edifice they build up, that is the *sa* and the *mandra saptak,* claims the greatest attention. Once the foundation is laid, the angles of the rising structure are gently indicated while the apex is often left to the imagination of the listener, in deference to the underlying philosophy that a mere human does not have the ability to perfect or complete anything, including the portrait of a raga.

The Athrauli-Jaipur gayaki of which Ustad Alladiya Khan was the champion is known for its sharply etched and brilliant *alankars* or note patterns. The typical presentational model of this gharana is to outline the entire bandish in medium tempo at the outset and then to embellish and underline the structure with scintillating patterns of rhythm and melody. The strength of this music lies not in the nuance of expression or emotion but in the fluency and the sparkling clarity and energy of the musical utterance which can be likened to a finely cut diamond.

The Patiala gayaki stresses the presentational aspect and achieves its effect through an exuberance of spirit and a sense of abandon. The music often takes the form of a series of build-ups and climaxes, where the musicality of the moment takes precedence over sense of structure.

There are many other gharanas and styles in addition to these. The point here is to recognise that each is the embodiment of an outstanding musical personality and each has the potential of attracting to itself like-minded music lovers. The riches of the minds of the masters who have given rise to such a wealth of styles in India can be likened to the immoveable property of the members of the gharana which includes their disciples as well. Another kind of wealth which each gharana owns and which we can consider their moveable property is the repertoire of compositions and ragas they specially pride themselves on. This wealth is as jealously guarded by all members who identify themselves with the gharana as any other kind of riches and shared only with those who are admitted into the family by right of blood, marriage or exemplary discipleship. By following both the manner and material of musical masters, their disciples give rise to a distinctive stream of musical practice.

The origins of the Kirana gharana go back a long way and include the contribution of luminaries like Bande Ali Khan, the legendary master of the *been*. Kirana is the name of a town near Saharanpur in Uttar Pradesh where the emperor Jahangir is said to have resettled many families of musicians after their homes were destroyed in a flood. Many sarangi and sitar players also trace their ancestry to this town. But the gayaki as we know it today is the product of two great musical minds—that of Abdul Karim Khan, and of his nephew Abdul Wahid Khan. Together they are considered the pillars of this musical legacy even though no two temperaments or personalities could be more different. While the uncle's forte was emotional appeal and delicate lyricism, the nephew's music was celebrated for its intellectual vigour, purity of raga and relentless sense of structure. Abdul Karim Khan overwhelmed the listener with feeling, while Abdul Wahid Khan challenged his mind to its limits. Both are capable of miraculous musical feats in their separate ways. The manner of these two masters was followed by their respective disciples, thus giving rise to two distinct sub-streams of musical practice within the Kirana school.

The story goes that at an informal family gathering, Abdul Karim Khan enchanted all those present with his rendering of the raga Mian-ki-Malhar. His concentration on tunefulness sometimes led him to take minor liberties with a raga. Only Abdul Wahid Khan's piercing mind detected that certain notes were being used in an unorthodox manner and that the purity of the raga as understood in the Kirana gharana was being compromised. He was severely critical at first but at the end of the concert, when he saw that the entire audience was spellbound, he remarked that Abdul Karim Khan's voice had indeed been blessed by divine grace and to find fault with his music was like challenging the Almighty.

THE TWO STREAMS OF A RIVER

Despite the seemingly wide differences in the musical manner of these two pillars of the Kirana gharana, their approach and concerns had much in common at a deeper level. What they shared distinguished them clearly from all other gharanas and was more vital and decisive than any physical dissimilarities could be. The common lineage that nurtured them had implanted in both their psyches an almost exclusive preoccupation with raga development. Both considered a sincere and penetrating search for *swara* more important than presentational aspects such as *taal* and ornamentation. Both chose depth over variety, suggestion over statement, quality over quantity, and the subtle and sophisticated over the overt and the obvious. Both shared the same concept of the unbroken melodic line which in the case of the Kirana gayaki arises from silence, stretches and gains body in an arc and fades back into silence, without any abrupt breaks, angles or jerks. For both the masters it is an article of faith that the exact place of a note in its surrounding aura has to be searched for and discovered anew every time a phrase is attempted. Its exact position cannot be taken for granted as though one had fixed it on the harmonium. Both masters are more attracted to the slow tempo than to the *drut* since the leisurely pace affords the opportunity to explore the contours of the raga in greater detail. Both demonstrate in their practice that concentration on a small musical area, whether it is a single raga, or three notes in it, is more rewarding than restlessly moving from raga to raga, or indiscriminately adding to one's collection of compositions. In deference to this conviction, both prefer to present serious ragas that have a rich development potential and are not usually attracted to sweet-sounding or popular ragas that do not seriously challenge the mind. This tendency can be seen in all singers of the Kirana school who specialise in profound creations like Todi, Yaman, Shuddha Kalyan, Puriya and Darbari and do not generally attempt easy-to-please ragas like Chayanat, Nand, Desh and Khamaj. Not only that: they tend to treat even a light raga with so much depth that it acquires new characteristics. Abdul Karim Khan's Abhogi Kanhra is a case in point. The original Karnatic raga that was the inspiration for it is beautiful and lyrical, but nowhere as profound and majestic as the conception of the raga envisioned by singers of the Kirana gharana.

Abdul Wahid Khan was once asked why he limited himself to only two ragas, Todi and Darbari, which he practised day in and day out. His response was that he would have dropped the second one too if morning time could last forever. One lifetime, according to him, was not enough to do justice to any raga. He was forced to change from Todi to something else only because of the setting sun and the gathering darkness.

The musical values that these two great masters held dear to their hearts in their own individual ways were broadly the same. All musicians of the Kirana school are aware of the two main streams that they represent within the same value system and consciously adhere to one or the other, or a combination of the two, in a proportion which is congenial to their musical personalities. They are also aware that despite superficial differences in manner, both streams address themselves to the same musical concerns. The similarities outweigh the differences and establish a common ancestry.

SUPREMACY OF SWARA

The Kirana gharana developed in response to a deep urge for personal self-expression. Masters like Abdul Karim Khan concentrated their entire attention on the poignance and nuance of the swara and did not make very active use of rhythm in creating the desired effect. The luminosity and exact placing of the swara in the raga became so important to the practitioners of this style that they laid themselves open to the charge by other gharanas of neglecting the tala and the bandish. In this sense the Kirana gharana was an unorthodox, even in some senses an erratic development. In order to give the utmost latitude to the alaap element which is the most evocative and emotive part of raga delineation, both Abdul Karim Khan and Abdul Wahid Khan reduced the tempo of the *bada khayals* to the slowest it had ever been in the history of the khayal. It was their conviction that the meditative, contemplative and emotional aspects of music which attracted them most could not possibly be coaxed out of music at a brisk pace. This development resulted in impressive feats of musicality at a very high level, and began to be imitated by other gharanas as a necessary condition for evoking feeling from a raga. Many performers of the Jaipur gharana, for instance, have now begun to preface their recitals with slow alaap in the Kirana mode which would have been unthinkable for them fifty years ago.

This is true of some other gharanas as well. In fact the walls of the gharanas have become more porous than they used to be and there is much unconscious borrowing and lending in a competitive spirit. With the greater access provided by electronic aids and increased physical mobility, there is much more exchange and contact, acknowledged and unacknowledged, between the gharanas and many examples of mixed gayakis are audible on concert stages today. The interesting fact is that today no singer or player of any school can resist the lure of the slow *badhat* which used to be the exclusive preserve of the Kirana school. Even those who point out that the emphasis given to this aspect is lopsided cannot but extend silent respect to the meditative *vilambit* and leisurely badhat of the Kirana style. The most conclusive and effective compliment to this speciality is that it is imitated across all frontiers of gharana or style and has gained not only acceptability but universal prestige. At the same time it must be admitted in fairness that some Kirana singers in their turn try to outdo the *tayyari* or fast singing which is a speciality of other gharanas and not their own forte in an effort to measure up and not be found wanting in any aspect. Even so, it is possible to distinguish the special traits that were originally contributed by the Kirana gharana.

THE MELODIC LINE AND SENSE OF STRUCTURE

One outstanding feature of the Kirana gayaki is the refined sculpting of the melodic line. The practitioners of the Kirana style tend to regard the entire scale as a continuous flow of musicality and not a series of separate notes. Conceptually, every phrase in a raga is represented by a flowing line which passes smoothly through all the gradations of the participating notes without revealing the joints. The extremely fine tuning of the intonation of the line conveys the emotional intention, subtly and enduringly, as though it were not a string of notes but a single musical sound with a distinct expression. In other words, the Kirana sensibility aspires to absorb the emotional ambience and aura of a particular limb of the raga instead of hearing a series of notes separately and literally. This gayaki abhors angles and abrupt breaks so that the continuity of the spirals that the voice traces is maintained. It is the unceasing effort of all practitioners to make this their second nature. Attention is given not only to where the melodic line originates and ends, but also to its thickness or thinness at any given point. This type of detailed and delicate calligraphy lends the music a third dimension of physical depth which is palpable to the ear.

Another speciality of the Kirana approach is that the raga is conquered not by treading relentlessly up and down its scale but by locating and controlling the crucial pressure points in its structure. For instance in most *sapoorna* ragas, an understanding of the function of the *nishadh* and the *madhyam*, or of *rishabh* and *dhaivata*, or of any two notes and their mutual relationship holds the key that could open the doors to the raga's innermost recesses. These are not accessible by mere force of practice. As a corollary to this way of looking at the raga, the typical Kirana singer fashions even his fast *taans* from a structural rather than an ornamental point of view, that is to say he takes into cognisance the vital organs and anatomy of the raga with a view to capturing its distinctive flavour and essence. He is not content merely with weaving attractive note patterns that may be pleasant to the ear. The progress of the perfect Kirana *taan* thus satisfies the connoisseur's sense of structure as much as, and sometimes even more than, his melodic expectations.

RESTRAINT AS A MUSICAL VALUE

Another area of subtlety is the use of silence and understatement as effective musical elements. The comparatively low-key sensibility of the Kirana singers is also expressed in their leisurely but meticulous attention to the *mandra saptak*. As we have already seen, the raga is developed note by note in the manner of a pyramid. The tempo of the music also rises as the structure progresses. When the apex of the pyramid, the *taar shadaja*, is reached, it is not punished overtly and repeatedly as in many other styles, but merely suggested, as though the music was being completed in the mind rather than physically. An example of this is found in the music of Amir Khan who adopted this attitude from the Kirana principles and carried it to an extreme because it admirably suited his introspective and meditative nature.

The cursory treatment of the *antara* in a bandish can be seen in the music of Abdul Wahid Khan. This indicates a preference for understatement and gesture over physical completeness. A mere pointer to the *taar saptak* which finally reveals the face of a raga can sometimes be more aesthetically satisfying to an evolved musical taste than an overt and detailed treatment of that area. Abdul Wahid Khan never repeated the antara on principle and preferred to position it in such a manner that it did not occupy the whole space of the *vilambit taal* cycle, usually the fourteen beat *jhoomra*, but accommodated itself within ten or eleven *matras*. It is well known that most traditional *vilambit khayal* compositions that have been handed down through this stream allow three or four beats to pass after the *sam* before the antara is taken up. The significance of this practice is only psychological in that it reflects a kind of restraint, and a faith that musically, suggestion and delicacy are more appealing than outright statement and mechanical reiteration.

All singers of the Kirana gharana share this conviction in their different ways and to varying extents. And yet each has an emphatic individuality. In fact, the test of a genuine gharana is not only that at least three generations must have upheld the tradition but also that each single exponent should be able to express his individuality and leave his personal stamp on the music. If this condition is not met, then the teaching is open to the charge of being nothing more than an opportunity to imitate. The gurus of the

Kirana gharana pride themselves on their ability to transmit the technique of the art so that their followers can distinguish their own musical urges from the mannerisms of their masters and still express them through the traditional idiom they have been taught. The success of their efforts is borne out by the fact that the music of each singer of the Kirana gharana reflects an original individual personality and not a stereotype.

Among the disciples Abdul Karim Khan groomed are Roshanara Begum, Ganesh Ramachandra Behere, Balakrishnabua Kapileshwari, Firoz Dastoor and Sawai Gandharva—who in turn trained Gangubai Hangal and Bhimsen Joshi. Each of these artists has a distinct style even though they adhere to the same principles. This also applies to Abdul Wahid Khan's star pupil Hirabai Barodekar, a daughter of Abdul Karim Khan, who in her turn became the idol of singers like Manik Verma and Prabha Atre. In the course of his stay in Lahore, the master also taught Jeevan Lal Mattoo, his son Jawaharlal Mattoo and his daughter-in-law Madhuri Mattoo. All three were lifelong practitioners. Another faithful pupil was Pran Nath who dedicated his entire life to upholding and popularising the style and musical attitudes of his guru. In the USA, where he spent the latter part of his life, he continued to teach the music of the Kirana school according to his lights and built up an extensive archive of recordings of compositions bequeathed to him by his master.

In general it can be said that the sub-stream represented by Abdul Wahid Khan is drier and more austere than the evocative and poignant manner of Abdul Karim Khan, but from the technical standpoint, the former is regarded more authoritative by most people. The attitudes of the two masters colour their musical expression also. The accents of Abdul Karim Khan are tender, full of love and go straight to the heart. It is said that he was greatly influenced by the feeling that *thumri* singers like Moijuddin Khan were able to evoke in their music. On the other hand, the utterance of Abdul Wahid Khan, though equally persuasive, was somewhat intimidating in comparison.

REFLECTIONS ON THE KIRANA LEGACY
PERCEPTIONS OF THE PRESENT GENERATION

The foregoing observations provide only a bird's-eye view of the trends that have been followed in the Kirana gharana. However, in the present generation, those who like me have been fortunate enough to study with Ustad Faiyyaz Ahmed and Ustad Niaz Ahmed of that gharana have had the chance to look more closely at this legacy and all that it implies. One of the most impressive elements in it is the teaching techniques that have been developed and perfected by these ustaads.

In musical matters, the two brothers seemed to have one soul, even though their bodies were separate. They communicated perfectly at many levels without having to use too many words. Apart from the natural affinity between brothers who have grown up and received their musical education in the same environment, they had common musical values as a matter of personal preference. They were inheritors of the same traditions and reacted to musical questions in the same way. For these reasons they were able to evolve a highly efficient method of teaching in which the labour involved was intelligently shared between the two of them. Each took responsibility for a different requirement in the grooming of a pupil. Generally, Faiyyaz Ahmed taught the nuances of the *chalan* of a raga and outlined the compositions while Niaz Ahmed ensured that the minutest details of each lesson penetrated deeply and became an inalienable part of the pupil's musical vocabulary. The elder brother enriched the teaching with extraordinary refinement of feeling, while the other brought to it an equally impressive discipline and devotion. But these roles could be interchanged if need be. However, for the most part the strong points of both were imaginatively made available to each student in the manner most advantageous to them.

The two ustads did not have a blanket prescription for all their students, but devised, most painstakingly, the best course of 'treatment' for every known musical 'malady'. Their diagnostic ability was also phenomenal. When I was first examined by them for possible discipleship, it took them no more than five minutes to discover that I had a tendency to be nasal, that my *meendh* was rough and jerky, that my pitches in the *aarohi* tended to be higher than in the *avarohi*, and that I lacked serenity. But they kept this bad report to themselves lest the disclosure shatter my self-confidence at the outset. Much later I was gently told about this only as a matter of interest, and only after these faults had been treated and corrected to the extent possible.

My lifelong experience with music teachers had led me to believe that teaching simply meant the opportunity to imitate. I realised only through Niaz Ahmed and Faiyyaz Ahmed that teaching music was a highly developed art, quite distinct from the the art of creating music but every bit as challenging. My teachers prided themselves on the teaching skills they had learnt in addition to and as distinct from their musical training. Their sincerity and inventiveness in this area was remarkable. I remember many feats that are still talked about among their students. They once cured a disciple who was chronically *kamsura* by holding up three parallel fingers every time she touched the *taar sa* and telling her that her voice had reached only as high as the first finger whereas she actually needed to pitch her voice to the third one. They gradually guided her ear and her psychology until she got her bearings and readjusted her ear to the right pitch. Another instance that comes to mind is that, once, they succeeded in correcting the inflection and intonation of a typical phrase in the raga Mian-ki-Malhar by telling a student to actually sing the *mandra saptak pa* while keeping her mind firmly on the *sa*! This took several hours of trial and error since it was not an old and tried remedy but one invented on the spot to solve an unexpected problem that had arisen.

It had been ingrained in Niaz and Faiyyaz Ahmed by their ustads and elders that the musical treasures they were in possession of were not their personal property but wealth which they held in trust and which it was their sacred duty to pass on to deserving aspirants. They did not merely pronounce this but actually lived it in their professional dealings. Their generosity in teaching was phenomenal. A lesson ended only when the pupil simply could not absorb any more.

The willingness to impart, which is in any case a rare quality in traditional circles, is not always matched by the ability to do so. In the case of this duo it was. Their teaching skills were of a very high order and were constantly fuelled by a bewildering variety of demands from their students. Each individual had a different problem for which corrective remedies had to be devised. Each had specific requirements and preferences so far as material was concerned. The two ustads who worked as a team saw to it that every student of theirs was satisfied and on the right track. They never gave up and never discouraged anybody lest it break their spirit. These human qualities and considerations were impressive considering that in matters of music the two brothers were absolutely uncompromising. Association with such teachers exposed their pupils not only to the finer points of music, but to an infectious value system that embraced both aesthetics and ethics.

MAULANA AND HIS BHAI SAHIB

The clean, disciplined and self-denying life style of Niaz Ahmed Khan earned him the title of Maulana. Not only his extended family, but the entire music world knows him by that epithet. His dedication to the purity and practices of the Kirana gharana is a matter of faith with him. But there are lesser known facets of his personality which occasionally surprise his devotees. His forté is a systematic and meticulous style of raga development, but he can on occasion render the most touching and emotional thumri in the vein of Abdul Karim Khan. He once ended a concert in Bombay with the famous *jamuna ke teer* in Bhairavi and there was hardly a dry eye in the hall when he finished. Some of us have even heard him sing a beautiful *dhun* he composed for a ghazal, in a rare light mood. He stopped in embarrassment when his elder brother happened to walk in accidentally, but everyone present, including his elder brother, was amazed at the range of his musical sensibilities.

The performance mode of the two brothers was quite different from the teaching one. One might well ask how two separate people can possibly express their innermost musical urges together, and yet this is exactly what they succeeded in doing. In fact, as performers they achieved more in partnership than they would have as individuals. They used their separate strengths as an advantage to extend the reach of their music. Each in turn securely held the frame of the structure they built up, leaving the other free to explore the furthest limits of his imagination. Faiyyaz Ahmed Khan skilfully and delicately filled in the colours of the raga, while Niaz Ahmed Khan animated it with brilliant embellishments and taan patterns. Neither would have been able to go as far as they did in their own preferred area of creativity but for the support and strength of the other. Fortunately for posterity, an example of their best work is available in a series of recordings by HMV. The Yaman recorded by the two brothers is a feat of musicianship which is universally acknowledged as a definitive interpretation of the raga and is still referred to and cited by aspiring singers.

There were some values which they stressed again and again and one of them was spontaneity. They seldom discussed or rehearsed what they were going to sing together. What they might thus have lost in physical slickness was more than made up by the freshness and genuineness of their expression. '*Nit naya*' was a constant ideal they followed. For them, nothing could be less desirable than stale musical cliches. They never encouraged their students to pre-plan their recitals, but always urged them to be true to the moment and listen to what the tuned tanpura seemed to be suggesting before deciding what they felt like singing.

The sculpting of the melodic line and the meendh was a constant concern for them. Every student was required to understand and observe their very strict rules about the movement of the line. They tirelessly explained how to raise a note, how to stay on it, how to leave it and how to travel to the next note. There were also very detailed principles that governed where the voice should apply force and where it should be allowed to drop by itself.

Their formulations were so strict that they used to remind us of the laws of gravity. The structural use of *kana* was another extremely important lesson that they tirelessly stressed and asked all their pupils to practise. They explained to us that the emotional expression of a musical phrase depended on the movement and conduct of a melodic line, including the *sut*, or fine thread of sound with which a musical phrase fades out, and so it was deserving of the most delicate attention. There were numerous such refinements in their teaching which they normally undertook separately, so that the pupil could concentrate better on the matter in hand. They were rarely present at a lesson together, unless there was a specific reason for it.

The compositions of Faiyyaz Ahmed Khan, or Gunarang, are very special and bear his unmistakeable stamp. They have the aroma of the graceful khayals of a bygone age and carry within them all the sensitivity and depth required for a complete grasp of the intention of a raga. For many listeners, these khayals used to be an added attraction at any concert of the two brothers. Even after his death in 1987, Niaz Ahmed Khan and some performing pupils continued to feature these compositions in their recitals as they are masterpieces in a distinctive style which one associates with the gayaki of the two brothers.

One quality which stands out in these compositions is that they do not lose their sense of repose, however accelerated the *laya* might be in the *drut*. Usually the exact pitches of the notes of a raga have to be sacrificed for the sake of speed and *tayyari*. Nor can the arches of the meendhs be faithfully traced in the fury of the increased tempo. This is not the case in the compositions of Maulana's beloved 'Bhai Sahib'. There are numerous examples. To pick some at random, his *drut ektal* compositions in Megh and Mian-ki-Malhar, or his *taranas* in Malkauns and Kausi Kanhra, are feats of musicianship as well as aesthetics which uphold the ancient values of purity and restraint. These compositions have been added to the repertoire of the common pool and are a living proof of the invaluable contribution of the two brothers to their inherited legacy.

It is rare indeed to find the highest standards of professional ability mingle so easily and comfortably with the broad sympathies and human qualities for which Niaz Ahmed Khan and Faiyyaz Ahmed Khan are so widely known. In our own cynical times, where self-interest and self-propagation seem to be the only surviving values, this might well be their most enduring and far-reaching contribution.

FOUR

The Cooking of Music

Interestingly, the term for classical music in everyday speech is '*pakka gana*', or music that has been subjected to the process of *pakana*, ripening or cooking. The Hindustani word *pakka* has a chequered history and has ended up in English dictionaries as 'pucka', meaning genuine, solidly built, of full weight, enduring, and therefore emphatically *not* ephemeral. In relation to music, the word is not just descriptive. It couches a thin layer of warning which seems to say this path is not for those looking for instant gratification. There is enough in the term and its associations to intimidate the prospective aspirant, however adventurous. The technical jargon used by professionals to fend off the casual and the merely curious is no help at all in making 'pakka gana' less forbidding to the outsider. 'Insiders' actually derive some satisfaction from the fact that common musical terms like *gharana, meendh, gayaki, samvadi,* and *abhog* are only their preserve and as unfamiliar as Greek to most other people. This esoteric aura coupled with the raucous, uninhibited singing voices of most ustads does not affect the listening pleasure of aficionados but jars on the ears of the uninitiated. I remember that as children (brats really) we used to take malicious pleasure in mimicking such voices as an act of heroic irreverence. But it was reassuring to be scolded for playing this insolent game because it confirmed that the seemingly harsh world of 'pakka gana', though not instantly enjoyable, must in some ultimate sense be good and valuable like religion and medicine.

A word that is commonly used in northern India in praise of music is *mazaa*, or enjoyment. This is a coarse version of the classical concept of *rasa* but its closest associations are with food, though it can be stretched to encompass other senses too. What the performing musician in the Indian classical tradition sets out to do is very similar to the aims of the chef. The dish must be prepared according to ancient recipes that have stood the test of time, it must be creative and carry the personal signature of the cook, it must preserve and serve the original flavours of the ingredients in all their freshness, it must ensure that all the spices and condiments come together in a single confection, and most importantly, the experience, the taste, the mazaa should live in the mind of the consumer, that it should be *pakka*—which is the chosen antonym for *kaccha*—meaning uncooked, weak, breakable, and fragile.

The lore of classical music gladly, even boastfully, accepts that this does not always happen, that things do not necessarily come together simply because the right recipe has been faithfully followed. In fact there is a common saying with which frustrated pupils are often consoled. '*Raag, rasoi, paagree, kabhi kabhi ban jaye,*' that is to say, perfection in presenting a raga, creating a culinary dish and tying the pagri cannot always be achieved. It is also well known that these are areas in which deliberate effort is likely to be counter-productive and that the crucial element in the success of such undertakings is an uncontrollable magic which works in mysterious ways.

The similarity between the two activities of producing music and producing food is quite compelling. Both rely more for their quality on spontaneity and the ruling instinct of the moment than on any rigid recipe. In both, the dish tastes different each time it is attempted and the sharing of its goodness is crucial to the endeavour in both cases.

However, there is a built-in technique in the classical tradition which ensures that the ineffable, delicate musical creation of the artist is not dependent on spontaneity alone. Conceptually, this technique owes quite a lot to the culinary field. The freshest green vegetable, if left in its pristine state indefinitely, loses its crispness, colour and fragrance. After a time, it becomes stale and finally begins to rot and smell bad. The only thing that can save it is pickling in brine or vinegar. This preserves its essential nature and flavour, but at a price. The immediacy, the raw taste of the artist's personal feeling, which is his alone, has to be sacrificed in the interests of durability and wider comprehension. Expressed in the language of the raga, the musician's emotion undergoes a process of distancing and a virtual rebirth. It is poured into a traditional mould and ideally emerges as an expression which is recognisable and universal, even though the imprint it bears is that of the individual artist.

Very roughly speaking, the way it works is this. Let us say that the musician at the time of performance feels inspired to paint a portrait of his anguish. He will then choose an appropriate raga, one that bears in its prescribed and approved structure the seeds of the anguish that musicians before him have felt for hundreds of years. Of course, his personal anguish cannot ever be exactly the same as that of the collective entity of the musical past we are talking about, but if he renounces tradition and goes it alone, so to speak, two dangerous things are likely to happen. One, that his original cry from the heart remains a cry in the wilderness and goes unheard because it does not use a language that anybody else can fully understand. Even if he manages to communicate the emotion he is experiencing, there is a second danger he faces. The emotion, since it has not been treated with any kind of preservatives, becomes stale and tiresome in the minds of his listeners after a while. Hundreds of examples of bad music come to mind where the main thing that has gone wrong is that powerful feelings have been directly aimed at the heartstrings without any distancing or 'cooking'. However beautiful or fragrant a musical idea may be at birth, it cannot retain its freshness and beauty unless it is treated in some fashion that guarantees long-term health. Leaning on the restraint and purity of the classical idiom usually achieves this end automatically.

What the performing musician does is to try and salvage the emotion he is experiencing from oblivion by translating it in the sturdy, and weatherproof vocabulary of an ancient musical language that people trust, understand and love. To go back to the anguish the musician wishes to express, he has a wide choice of ragas he can use for the purpose. He will pick a suitable one much as one picks out the clothes one feels like wearing on a particularly sad day. Most ragas that use *komal* or flattened *re* and/or *dha* (for instance, the Todi family, or Bhairavi, or Asavari) would normally fit the bill.

The fact that the ragas as they exist at present relate to what someone else has felt at one time does not necessarily imply that today's performer must slavishly echo the feelings of masters who have gone before him. It only means that he is processing his creative urge and using the raga he has chosen as a blueprint to work on so that he can truly share the outcome which still remains his personal statement. There is an apocryphal but serviceable story that when Tansen died, his son Bilas Khan mourned him by singing a Todi which was a spontaneous variation of something his father had composed. This new raga, one of the most mournful of creations, was given the name Bilaskhani Todi and won a place of honour in the repertoire of Hindustani musicians. During the last three hundred years or so, it has been sung and played by every single master of every gharana and no two renditions are even faintly alike. Each is an original musical portrait, though it embodies a poignancy that someone else first felt and expressed many years ago. The model only provides a frame of reference, a sort of common musical language. It certainly does not dictate in a manner that might snuff out creativity.

My experience is limited to the luminaries and musical ustads of the north Indian heartland. I have never encountered one to whom the cooking and serving of good food was not extremely important. Granted that in India, as in most poor countries, feeding is the most obvious way of expressing love and concern. But in the life styles of the personalities I am thinking of, it has a slightly different cultural resonance. It is a symbol of the desire to create exquisiteness and to allow the more favoured or less privileged to bask in it. There is a faint suggestion of princely generosity, of *mabadaulat*, in most such gestures and they are so graceful that it is invariably a pleasure to be at the receiving end.

When Zia Moinuddin Dagar travelled to New York to stay with an ardent American disciple, the first thing he did was to take charge of the kitchen and start operations on the lamb *qorma* so that it would be ready by the time the first day's music session ended. Only then did he settle down to tune his *rudra veena*. The lesson progressed while the dish slowly cooked. Throughout the day, he would periodically rise from his instrument to peer into the pot intently and stir it a bit. The ardent disciple ended up learning at least as much about Mughlai cooking as about raga and playing technique. Within twenty days the resident smells of Italian sausage, spaghetti sauce, and oregano in the old Manhattan apartment yielded unconditionally to the more authoritative odours of coriander, cumin and garam masala. The ustad confirmed that the tone and pitch of the pupil had simultaneously become so much more satisfactory that it was time to have a combined food and music feast for all friends and acquaintances.

This is indicative of a way of life that was common to most musicians in northern India. Pandit Pran Nath used to say that real music was only for those who could replicate the aroma of kababs in every note. Bade Ghulam Ali Khan once announced to an inadequate host that he could hardly be expected to produce his kind of music if he was given grass to eat. '*Ai khana, te ai gana?*' he had exclaimed in shocked tones when he viewed the watery vegetables he had been served. Ustad Faiyyaz Ahmed Khan's favourite topic, next to ragas, was the culinary creativity of his wife. He took every opportunity to display her many wondrous feats as often and to as many people as he could. Every disciple, colleague, and acquaintance waited eagerly for the next culinary celebration in his home. Himmat Nivas, Munnawar Ali Khan's mansion in Bombay, was also a legendary centre of hospitality and good eating. Siddheshwari Devi was an inspired cook and a compulsive feeder of all and sundry, just as she was in the way she served her music to her audience.

So was Begum Akhtar, though she was somewhat more discriminating. Her invitation to me to visit her in her home in Lucknow was prefaced with a promise to treat me to special kababs for which the neighbouring village of Kakori was famous. Of her recollections, the most graphic were descriptions of the cuisine of the princely state of Rampur, specially the *biryani* and the *badaam ki jaali*. The kinship between food and music, at least in the nawabi tradition of northern India, is undeniable. I have heard it said many times by ustads, '*Ek hi baat hai,*' meaning that both deal with regaling the senses with refinement, both endeavour to heighten the impact of taste, aroma, and ambience, and that both promise a feeling of repleteness.

This leads to the very large and open question of taste, of what will satisfy whom. Some people prefer *bhindi* to *karela*. Some prefer sweet to sour. No value judgement is possible here, and nothing is better or worse than anything else. But while retaining one's individual taste, it is possible to aspire to higher levels of enjoyment. If one likes sweet things, sugar by itself is no treat. The sensation of sweetness has to be carried to its furthest possibilities for it to make an enduring impact on the sensibilities of the listener. Once one has tasted the delights of bitter chocolate, it is difficult to return to the uncomplicated pleasure of one's first *rasagulla*. There are many ragas which do not sound delicious at first hearing (for instance Pat Bihag, Shiv Kalyan and many others), but the ear can be nurtured to a stage of sophistication where it acquires a taste for refinements like spices, black coffee, pickles, and caviar.

FIVE

Fear of Recording
The Non-Westernness of Hindustani Music

The Indian mind—and there is such a thing—has never taken kindly to the idea of formal records or, to stretch a point, to the activity of recording. It is well known that for this reason formal history was virtually unknown in the country until outsiders who had more faith in factual correctness than in philosophical generalisations took a hand. The chronicles of ancient India were often just impressionistic and fanciful accounts that gave as much weight to myth, prophecy, hyperbole and romance as to fact. But the total impression they conveyed was perhaps closer to the underlying reality than any listing of events. I cannot help feeling that there is an indigenous, Indian way of looking at things, of stepping back, squinting at the view and screwing up the eyes in an effort to spur the senses to inhale the essential truth of what is presented and to reject or discard the merely literal in the belief that it can veil or distort reality. Essence is a lazy and tricky word but it is useful in that it gives the instinct time to stall until exactly the right note has been sounded and one's whole being can say yes, this is it. In many important matters, certainly in music, reality is seldom the sum of its parts. The blue colour of the sky is not the result of contributions by a number of elements. On the contrary. No single element that enters into the physics and chemistry of our perception of the sky's blueness is in itself blue. Something of this sort holds good even more strongly for Indian music in general. In any case, it is difficult to talk about music without resorting to analogies. There is no other way, for music is its own justification and can speak of nothing but itself.

Since Indian music focuses less on the physical perfection of sound than other systems of music do, it follows that the concept of recording music cannot have the same associations and purposes. Or the same import either. It is sometimes easier to arrive at an understanding of Indian classical music by starting at the wrong end and eliminating all the things that it is not meant to be. First, it does not aim to please the ear by falling pleasantly on it. It does not tell a story or describe changing moods. It is neither the innermost personal expression of an individual sensibility, nor just an effort to interpret an ancient and rigid tradition—though it undeniably includes elements of all these. However meticulous and faithful the recording of an artist, a single occasion in the studio cannot yield a fair example of his work, because this music comes alive only in the process of improvisation and is never pre-planned or scored. We can compare it to the dying art of conversation which would cease to be just that if it were carefully planned or written down beforehand. Electronic recording inevitably involves the sort of pre-planning that cannot help changing the nature and intent of Indian classical music. That is why the best recordings today generally represent the poorest material while the best music available is usually embedded in recordings of such indifferent quality that one can hardly decipher it.

In the case of a Western composer, a recording celebrates the perfection and completeness of a scored work. It is a single, clearly projected musical statement. The differences in the interpretation of different conductors and players on different occasions are a matter of detail and largely at the level of nuance. The recording stands for all time as a reference point, as a musical monument, an almost permanent structure through which the listener can always unfailingly gain access to the musical awareness of the composer at the time he created the piece. This is not true of Indian classical music where the most valuable element to be celebrated is the fluidity, and the genuinely unpremeditated nature of the musician's utterance. The difference between the two is of kind, not of worth. If one is a perfectly structured sonnet, the other is spontaneous conversation which has no predetermined aesthetic goal. The level of wizardry in the two examples could be the same but it would always be located in different areas.

Imagine the raga to be an incense stick with a particular perfume. Every time the musician lights it, wisps of smoke arise from it in configurations that change continuously and cannot be foreseen even though they carry the recognisable perfume of the raga that is being presented. This spiral of melodic lines that can emanate from the incense stick of the raga can never be the same on any two occasions. The designs formed by the rising spirals of smoke are part of the ambience and certainly engage the listener, but arbitrarily recording any one of these moving lines and treating it as though it represented the whole musical intention of the artist can be misleading.

Of course the listener responds to the specific piece that is being performed but that is by no means the only source of his pleasure during a recital. The connoisseur's ear is automatically trained on other attendant skills the performer inevitably betrays without directly displaying them. For instance, his skill in articulation and the quality of his ambassadorship of the musical lineage he represents. These are crucial to the enjoyment of Indian listeners. The particular piece that is being performed is not considered a finished work of art by either the musician or his listeners. It is only an occasion for the artist to take his audience on exciting musical journeys which are effortlessly different each time he performs, even if it is the same raga or the same composition. That being the situation, the recording of any given piece is like taking a still photograph of a moving, palpitating animal. It is useful and valuable undoubtedly, but a mere stance. That obviously cannot be a substitute for the real thing. At best a recording can only capture what is called the *andaaz* of an artist, which means the particular flavour of their personal manner. The music itself arbitrarily represents only one of countless possibilities. It is an indication of an artist's potential, not his total creation in the sense in which a fully notated and scored work could be. Actually, the recording of a piece of Indian classical music says less than it leaves unsaid. And it is the unsaid that is more relevant to the pleasure of both listener and performer. By that I mean the bouquet, the flexibility implied in each musical statement, the luxurious sense that each could be said in infinite ways, the thrilling and urgent awareness of the living moment in which music is made in the form of an intimate personal communication. I suppose elements in this category would be considered valuable in all music but in the case of Indian music, where skill in improvisation is the real heart of the matter, they form at least three-fourths of the cake. As such a recording is as satisfactory or unsatisfactory as a clue. It is no more than that.

What we hear in a perfect recording of Beethoven's Fifth Symphony is certainly not just a clue to the genius of the composer. It is a creation which is complete in itself, a masterpiece which needs no additional exposure of any sort to make its full impact. The same is not true of say a recording of Raga Darbari by a maestro like Krishnarao Shankar Pandit. The recording of a single piece in his case would be no more than a sample of an extraordinary musical creativity. What the listener appreciates in these two specific cases is not comparable at all because the two are not immediately accessible to the same degree. The Indian example cannot be received by the listener with the same sense of completeness unless he first familiarises himself with the work and the vocalisation of Krishnarao Shankar over a period of time, the longer the better. Only then is there a chance that the listener can grasp the totality of the musical intent and accord to the Indian piece the level of admiration it is entitled to, a level which the Western piece, being complete in itself, commands without any annotation or footnotes. The achievement of the Indian piece is that it carries and imparts a sense of infinitude in the literal sense. Fluidity and freedom are inherent in any utterance in this tradition and there could be infinite possibilities of musical intention. That is what is valued most and for this reason it has to be accepted that any recording is bound to be a limiting thing since it arbitrarily captures only one face of the artist's conception of what he is trying to portray and misses several important dimensions. What is more, it wrongly implies that the face that has been captured is the whole being—as it indeed is in the case of the Fifth Symphony.

When the idea of recording first penetrated the Indian music world in the second decade of the twentieth century, it was regarded with the same mixture of distrust and fascination that any import from the West receives in our culture. Many of the pillars of the music world succumbed to the fascination and lure of immortality and there was a spate of 78 RPM discs which are invaluable today. But these examples, in which masters of the art have managed to condense two-hour performances into two and a half dazzling minutes, are like a collection of exquisite swatches of weaves presented in commercial houses to prospective buyers. One can revel in their beauty and marvel at the skill and resourcefulness which make such presentations possible, but there is no getting away from the fact that these recordings are not great feasts in themselves but only tasting opportunities, and in each case conclusive proof of the existence of wonderful cuisines.

Cultural collisions can produce anomalies of various kinds and the Indian attitude to recording, like the Indian attitude to American blue jeans, is one. I give this example because it is easy to understand. The young in India took to jeans like ducks to water, but they misunderstood or disregarded the underlying philosophy that went with the faded colours, torn edges and patches. For a good ten years jeans remained the preserve of the affluent and fashionable few. Young women were often seen alighting from expensive cars in high heels proudly sporting their ragged jeans, while deferential uniformed chauffeurs held the car door open for them. The mincing walk and the helpless manner of these women suggested that they regarded their attire as a status symbol, which is precisely what it was supposed to neutralise. The advent of the recording industry in India is a comparable phenomenon, in the sense that it gave rise to similar attitudinal confusions in the music community. Ripples of excitement at the novelty of the idea alternated with serious misgivings about the harmful effects of electrical gadgetry on the voice. It is widely known that many of the artists who succumbed to the temptation of recording in the 1920s and early 1930s feared that at the very least their work could be stolen and passed off as someone else's. This is why many of the old 78s end with the artist shouting out his name urgently and somewhat nervously in the naïve belief that this would be a safeguard against plagiarism and pirating. Many of them were sure that even worse things could happen to them. For instance, the microphone if given a chance could secretly siphon off all the goodness and power of their voice, just as making soup out of meat and vegetables robs them of their nutrients.

It took more than a decade of exposure and gentle persuasion by knowledgeable and caring people for this resistance to be overcome. But then, gradually the pendulum swung to the other extreme. Being recorded began to be considered the most prestigious thing that could happen to a performer. The more snobbish of the wives and mothers in families of musicians lost no opportunity to announce to less privileged rival groups that Khan Sahib was hardly ever at home these days because of the demands of 'rekartin'. By the 1940s and 1950s opportunities and openings to record for commercial companies and the radio were universally sought after, even though the format which recording studios demanded of musicians was strange and inhospitable. The physical placing of percussion and other accompaniment naturally gave precedence to the requirements of electronics rather than to the accustomed rapport between the musicians, which is the life of any performance. It was a daunting experience if not an ordeal for a singer to sit far away from his tabla and sarangi and still be able to warm up, as in a live concert. But this was one uncomfortable artistic situation most of them resigned themselves to in the hope of larger audiences and immortality. In any case, from being something new-fangled that was resisted on principle, recording became the new status symbol, like American blue jeans, and introduced a shift in the traditional attitudes to classical music.

FEAR OF RECORDING

Recording does play a crucial role in the Indian music world although it is a different kind of recording. Our music could not have evolved to the degree to which it has without preserving in some form the achievements of the past. An awareness of what has gone before or of what succeeding generations are building upon is crucial to the health of any tradition. It is a constant reference point which safely anchors the perception of both musician and listener in such a manner that further creative explorations and experiments can be based on it without endangering the entire structure. In fact recordings of all significant work done in the field are constantly in use, even though they are not electronic recordings but only recordings that exist in the mind. This is not surprising considering that we are talking about an oral tradition in which nothing is transmitted by any other means. It must be stressed that these 'mental recordings' of great masters form the heart of musical awareness in India and exercise a far greater influence on creative activity than any physical records could possibly do. That is not all. They are transferred to every succeeding generation of musicians and listeners, so that the process of evolution and enrichment remains continuous. The inheritors of the tradition not only reproduce it but recreate it anew each time, according to the demands of this art. The great advantage of this form of recording in musical lore and collective memory is that the present generation of performers can still be nourished and inspired by giants who were never recorded electronically. There are countless examples of this phenomenon.

There is hardly any passable recording of legendary names like Abdul Waheed Khan of the Kirana gharana, or Aman Ali Khan of the Bhendibazar gharana, or Rajab Ali Khan of the Gwalior gharana. But every serious music lover today is familiar with their style and accents because faithful imprints in the music of their devotees have been acclaimed by a core of older listeners who have heard the originals and shared their perceptions with the next generation. This happens on a very large scale and as a matter of course, much as the features and traits of a grandson can be likened to an ancestor whose spitting image he is reputed to be. I have never heard Aman Ali Khan but still have a pretty good idea of his style because all reliable ears in the music world recognise and point out that Shiv Kumar Sharma in his prime was a perfect clone. I am also familiar with the music of Abdul Waheed Khan and Abdul Karim Khan because of living musical contact with those who knew their music intimately. Admittedly this cannot be the same as actually having heard them but for the purposes of continuity and inspiration this kind of indirect transmission has proved to be immensely valuable. Today I can hear the three masters I have mentioned to my heart's content in the singing of a much recorded artist like Amir Khan and, what is more, distinguish the individual contribution of each to his style. Amir Khan based his life work on these three models though he forged a perfectly integrated new style of his own which he called the Indore gharana. The well-known Kumar Gandharva was deeply affected by the music of Onkar Nath Thakur of his own Gwalior gharana and the emotive utterance of Abdul Karim Khan of the Kirana gharana. Onkar Nath in an earlier generation was clearly affected by Rahmat Khan of the Gwalior gharana whose accents and style are preserved in the collective unconscious and the lore of the music world. One can hear Vilayat Khan, the sitar maestro, in the Darbari rendering of the sarod player Amjad Ali Khan, and Amir Khan in his Bilaskhani Todi. It is quite common during a concert for the audience to enjoy and point out similarities with earlier masters and to give credit to absent donors. The manner of Roshanara Begum, Hirabai Barodekar, Akhtari Bai, and Siddheshwari Devi is still imitated indirectly by aspiring women singers. The imprint of the vocalisation of Kumar Gandharva on the singing of Kishori Amonkar, Veena Sahasrabuddhe, and even Malini Rajurkar is unmistakeable, especially in the bhajans, though each achieves a creative transformation of her own. Despite the re-creation which is an important part of this type of transmission, the sources of the streams are clearly recognised by all concerned. The other day a brilliant young vocalist, recording her first CD, honoured the master she admired most simply by singing in his special manner. Everyone present recognised the tribute without a word having been said. 'I just felt like writing a love letter today', she remarked later.

Almost each time Mallikarjun Mansur sang Raga Jaunpuri, he would interrupt himself to tell his listeners that he was singing the *antara* in the characteristic manner of Manji Khan, a guru whom he adored. After a few minutes of demonstrating this, he would stop again to add that Manji Khan in his turn had got it from Rahmat Khan, an old master of an earlier generation whom Mallikarjun himself had probably never heard. Sharing his pride and joy at this rich lineage with his audience was often the high point of the concert. In this tradition no great musician lives alone on the creative mountaintop. That is not considered an ideal either. In a sense, all outstanding achievement in this field is collective, and there is a sense of participation by a warm, closely connected joint family which lives in the mind of the musician and provides him with all the earlier recordings he might wish to refer to. In fact a sense of identification with what has gone before is so much a part of the culture of this tradition that it almost enters the music as a value.

SIX

Sunlight in the Raga

My friend Nalin had a dubious project he was very earnest about. Every Sunday morning, he used to play selections from his favourite Indian classical music for the benefit of American acquaintances whom he hoped to convert. His much admired and very expensive sound system occupied most of his tiny mid-town Manhattan apartment. The handful of people he managed to lure to these sessions sat on floor cushions, eagerly awaiting enlightenment and spiritual enrichment. The staying power of the enthusiasts was erratic, so there was a new lot every week. Even so, the host was happy to guide the listening of those present, confident that he was opening for them doors to undreamed-of celestial spaces, spiriting them as far away as possible from the brutal Monday-to-Friday global investment business routine in New York City in which he himself was hopelessly enmeshed. He was convinced that the slow, meditative *khayal* was the surest remedy for the jangled nerves and fractured minds that led most of his American friends routinely to the couch of the psychoanalyst.

Into this set-up entered Beatrice, a Wall Street colleague, with whom Nalin was in the process of getting romantically involved. He viewed her as a possible 'life partner' and for Nalin it was vital that a prospective spouse be as impressed with the greatness of Indian music as he himself was. He confided in me and asked me to help him in communicating with the Sunday group, with special attention to Beatrice. I was an old hand at all this, being a jaded veteran of wordy sessions called seminars by various arty outfits I was in touch with.

The first item on the agenda was the relationship between the north Indian ragas and the time of day when each could appropriately be heard. I droned on in a practised way about the relevance of both Nature and the human condition to the mood of the music. I had had to do this kind of thing countless times in my career. But today, as young Beatrice twinkled with interest and tossed her bright yellow curls excitedly, I felt rewarded. She was positively incredulous when I added that the physical quality of the musical sound was not as important as what the music said, and that our most famous singers could be, and often were, eighty-year-old asthmatics with a permanent wheeze. Twelve people were intrigued enough to promise to turn up at dawn the following Sunday in order to listen to morning ragas at the prescribed hour, starting with Lalit, the first raga in the diurnal cycle.

Five of the twelve actually arrived. To Nalin's relief, Beatrice was among them. We started with one of our most treasured archival recordings of an old master from the Gwalior school. I was so solicitous of Beatrice that almost immediately, my own hearing broke into two distinct channels. The messages my brain was receiving through the left ear tallied with what I was used to, but the right ear seemed to be doing the listening on behalf of Beatrice. When I transferred the rough and weighty voice of the eighty-year-old master from my mind to where I imagined Beatrice's to be, it became a hoarse echo coming from a dark, bottomless well where nothing much seemed to be happening. 'Wait! Be patient! It *will* happen, I promise you!' I screamed silently, but the fact that she was fidgety, and thrashing her jeans-clad legs around, confirmed that even with the best will in the world she could not receive the perceptions I thought I was trying so desperately to beam in her direction.

The recorded master took his time with the comprehensive *alap*, the composition in slow tempo, the *jod* section, the *drut*, the *bol tan* and the fast *tan*. As he warmed up, the raucous vocal flourishes (which were only the outer garb of the divine music, as I had ritually warned the assemblage earlier) became bolder and more frequent. Beatrice could not believe the sounds she was hearing and was soon totally at sea. The well-intentioned Nalin was clearly oblivious to the effect his idols were having on his friends. As the music finally died down a good forty-five minutes later, he took over the commentary and requested the listeners to notice that this raga did not use the *pancham* or the fifth because that note represented the sun, and in this particular raga of the dawn, the sun had not yet risen. 'All *sandhi-prakash* ragas or ragas meant for the time when darkness meets light are sombre and mystical', he said, his eyes swimming with devotion. 'We will now go on to Todi, another meditative and serious raga of the morning. When the sun can be seen on the horizon, it is time for Todi and that is why this raga allows the pancham or perfect fifth in its scale'. 'Oh, no. Not another one!' the horrified Beatrice gasped. Nalin, engrossed in sliding an LP worshipfully out of its sheath, did not register her response.

Two of the five people in the group that morning hurriedly departed before the second item could unfold. I could see that Beatrice was tempted to join them, but steeled herself to stay on. She really liked Nalin. He was now putting on the music, eyes half closed in reverence. This time a master of the Agra gharana rendered all the labyrinthine stages of the raga, taking all of fifty minutes. I was full of admiration for the singing but half of me could not help listening as though I was Beatrice. The stentorian, rasping voice did really sound like furniture being shifted on a stone floor. Without the magic key which Beatrice did not yet have, the piece was a dull and claustrophobic exercise, a realistic representation of a slowly winding underground tunnel at the end of which there was only more darkness and confusion. When the Todi was over, Nalin sighed and nodded his head with deep satisfaction.

'This brings us to Jaunpuri, the third morning raga, which is performed when the sun is a little higher on the horizon, just beginning to light up the sky. But the feeling in the melody is still one of wistfulness and longing ...' began Nalin, trying faithfully to track the musical day of traditional India living itself out according to the rules of the game. Beatrice could not contain herself any longer. 'Doesn't your day *ever* pick up?' she burst out, staring at her watch in disbelief. She collected her things hurriedly and rushed out, mumbling incoherent apologies. Nalin looked stricken and shocked at the same time. Naturally, the budding romance quickly withered after this episode.

Beatrice was borne away from both my life and Nalin's on a meditative Jaunpuri note, but the concept of the sun in the pancham stayed to haunt me periodically. It was not something that had newly occurred to me during Nalin's fateful listening session. None of the dozen teachers I had learnt from over the years had ever articulated it to me clearly as a theory, but it must have somehow seeped in through an unconscious channel and stayed with me like an item of incidental luggage. Now that Beatrice had taken away with her body the distracting first part of my double role of interpreter and connoisseur, it made even more sense. In Lalit, the raga of the dawn which we had played first, the pancham was conspicuously absent, like a strong opinion deliberately not stated. The raga released its expression only when the two madhyams below it and the delicate *komal dhaivata* above it wove elaborate tonal patterns around the area where the pancham, representative of the sun, would normally have been placed had it existed at all in the scale of Lalit. As it was, the entire raga seemed to be inspired by the night's longing for the morning, notwithstanding the urgently clanging fire engines and the gruff howls of the ambulances in the street below, competing for the listener's attention.

'It makes all the difference to the mood of a sandhi prakash raga whether it is darkness turning into light, or light fading into darkness', I remembered one of my teachers saying long ago when the statement had meant nothing to me. I had taken it as the deliberate mystification that pliers of the musical trade in India delight in intimidating their dependents with. Now, thirty-odd years later when I genuinely felt the freshness of the morning air in a sun-less raga like Lalit, I was suddenly ashamed of my early scepticism. The late night raga Malkauns, which also omits the pancham, is every bit as dark as Lalit, but this darkness is quite different. For one thing it feels like an end rather than a beginning, an experience of depth that suggests magic and mystery, with no intimations of the coming day. Further the sense of the melody is, for want of a more accurate term, erotic. The *rasa* sought to be evoked is *shringara*, not philosophic devotion or bhakti as in Lalit, though the texts of some later compositions show a cavalier disregard for the natural bent of these ragas. Even marginal listeners are familiar with a well-worn Tulsidas bhajan in honour of Rama that has been beautifully and successfully set to the romantic Malkauns. Similarly, a description of cavorting maidens spraying colour and throwing flower garlands at besotted spectators is the subject of a much sung composition in the introspective strains of the ethereal Lalit! Incredible as it may seem, the results of such license can sometimes be so unexpected as to be truly wondrous, like a combination of colours that has never been seen.

Though Beatrice was long gone, the ear with which she had tried (and failed) to listen to Nalin's music stayed with me. I found myself scanning the diurnal arrangement of the ragas in Hindustani music like a tourist, pouncing gleefully on the slimmest evidence of a relationship between the strength of the pancham in a raga and the brightness of the sun in the sky at the corresponding hour. Bhairav was a perfect example. The fact that it was a morning raga was proclaimed by the fully manifested pancham, the risen sun, even though its positive rays in this raga seemed to be framed by the delicate greys of the *komal hrishabh* and the *komal dhaivata* in deference to the earliness of the hour. As the day progressed, these two notes in the raga clock tended to rise from their prostrate position to their full height as *shuddha* notes, either one at a time as the *re* alone in Jaunpuri, or together, as both the *re* and the *dha* in the fully lit Sarang family of ragas which unquestionably belongs to the noon. These were highly exciting observations for me, bringing back resonances of pedagogic voices I had never understood during my early training. Now a pattern seemed to be emerging. I actually experienced at first hand that the behaviour of the notes did have an organic connection with the time of day and the state of Nature. Although this had been instilled into me indirectly by a procession of teachers over the years, I had never really believed it until now.

However, there was still a problem. The more deeply I surveyed the scene, the more exceptions I found to my personal revelations about the time theory of ragas. This was unnerving. If the sages have a reason why the *re* and *dha* should be *komal* in morning ragas, why is this not so in Bilaval, I wondered. For each raga that fell neatly into place in the clock, there was at least one which suggested just the opposite, nipping all my enticing formulations in the bud. Still, the idea that the ragas in some way reflected the time of day was too alluring to abandon. I justified my position with the thought that most things Indian are made up of such widely varying strands that nothing one can say is wholly true or wholly false. Besides, the pristine state of nature can hardly ever have been a realistic background for any listener, especially for today's listener. Could anyone, in natural circumstances, ever have heard the sombre morning ragas without having to block out the shrill cries of the *kabariwala* and the vegetable hawker who have equal rights on that time of day?

Such unwelcome thoughts had been indirectly bequeathed to me by the Beatrice phenomenon. However hard I tried, I could not erase the memory of her imperviousness to what was in a sense my religion. She appeared like a phantom whenever I tried to connect music with the time of day, inextricable, like chewing gum in my hair. Jaunpuri, instead of evoking a late morning hour, conjured up for me images of Beatrice jogging in Central Park after fleeing Nalin's apartment. Busy and frenzied afternoon ragas like Multani and Patdeep became the backdrop for shopping at Bloomingdales. The time for the serene Kalyans of the evening was, I was sure, when she walked her dog. Durga was a short drink at a mid-town bar, and Bihag a leisurely dinner at an Italian restaurant in Soho. This was a hopeless state of affairs. I simply had to rid my mind of Beatrice so that I could get back my lost world of music.

To this end, I sought out Alaka, a nostalgic exile whose enthusiasm for Indian classical music bordered on insanity. I began to do all my listening in her company, in the hope that she would reinfect me back to my original state. She was a guaranteed antidote. In my more responsible moments, I suspected that the remedy was worse than the ailment, but on the whole I preferred it to the virus of scepticism. Needless to say Alaka was not a discriminating listener. She was just passionately in love with all ragas. Not only that. She indulged in deep affairs of the heart with individual notes. At this stage of our association, the object of her adoration happened to be *madhyama*, the fourth interval. 'It is velvety, dark blue, so rich, so mesmeric!', she breathed shyly, as though she was reluctantly sharing a secret about a lover. 'Let's listen to something that really celebrates its wonderful sound,' she pleaded with a touch of possessiveness, as though the note was her personal discovery if not her own creation. So we selected a vintage Kedara. When the raga developed enough to reveal the madhyam and came to rest on it, we exchanged involuntary glances in recognition of her passion for the note. At this point she actually blushed like a self-conscious schoolgirl. Her obsessions were clearly even more arbitrary than mine. This was dangerous territory and all the road signs I could see were unreliable. There was nothing for it but to return to a solitary state of listening and come to my own conclusions which were probably located in the wide space between the positions of Beatrice and Alaka.

I reminded myself that my favourite note was *sa*, named *shadaja* because it gives birth to the other six notes in the heptad and notionally embodies them all. Every teacher had told me that the melodic line approaching the *sa* should be so accurately and sensitively drawn as to reveal the entire raga. This became my new guideline for assessing the musicians I heard, though I still tried to relate the ragas to the time of day. I had been saturated with morning ragas at Nalin's sessions, so I now turned my attention to the evening ragas. I saw that they trace their slow way from failing light to gradually deepening darkness, travelling in the opposite direction from the sandhi prakash ragas of the morning. When the day is done, it is once again time for reflection and meditation as in the morning. An evening raga like Puriya Dhanashri, for instance, evokes a similar mood. It is lit up with the glowing pancham of the setting sun, but the *komal re* and *komal dha* in combination tone down the brilliance in anticipation of the gathering darkness. The difference is the entry of the *teevra madhyama*, the sharp raised fourth note, just a little below the pancham. This note is sounded strongly, without any undulation, pulling strongly away from the pancham and thus introducing a kind of tension usually not encountered in morning ragas. The interplay between these two notes determines the mood and character of many ragas that suggest twilight. A specially interesting raga for the time when the sun dips below the horizon is Marwa. Here also the sun or pancham disappears as in its morning counterpart Lalit. Both ragas are full of yearning, and depend heavily for their effect on the physical silence of this note, which though never sounded in either raga is nonetheless overwhelmingly present as a concept in both. The omission or sparing use of a strong note which could serve as a resting place in the development of a raga is a technique which is sometimes used with telling effect. Marwa is an interesting instance of this. Here, the tonic *sa*, though not altogether absent like the *pa*, is nonetheless elusive in most of the raga's phrasing. Normally a primary resting place, the *sa* is held back by design in this twilight raga in order to express its restlessness and agony.

The Kalyan family of ragas enters the field when the day's activity has subsided. Here the pancham in consonance with the serene *shuddha gandhar* ushers in a characteristic tranquillity. In this group, pancham is no longer king, so to speak, and has to share its radiance with *gandhar*, which acts as a competing satellite. Gradually the darkness deepens, inviting elements like mystery, grandeur and romance. Malkauns, the Kanhra family, Bihag and

Bageshri are typical examples of late night ragas. In the first, the pancham is omitted altogether. In the others, it abandons its literal role as the sun but contributes light with much greater delicacy and subtlety than in the morning ragas. And so it goes on through the night, until dawn breaks once more.

An awareness of the diurnal cycle has stayed with me in all my listening and performing, like a second skin. I still do not know whether it has any real basis or whether it is just an attractive notion I want to cling to. There can never be a final verdict on the time theory of ragas which I can accept without being plagued by the demons of doubt. To really know the truth, I need the visceral experience of listening in the company of an improved model of Beatrice, preferably in a new avatar.

SEVEN

Begum Akhtar

To my ears, the sound of the Urdu language and the ghazal were most enticing when I was in my teens even though I could not understand most of the words. I had no idea that the couplet had a form, and that it was necessary to tune in to the conventions of the ghazal to truly appreciate it. We studied Hindi and English in school and spoke a broad, not very elegant Hindustani at home. But, despite my ignorance, the recitation of a ghazal always transported me to a romantic world of make-believe which I preferred to all others. The heartbreak of unrequited love, the incredible selflessness of the lover who gloried in the pain that connected him to the beloved, the perfumed gardens where the rose and the bulbul conversed, about life and the spinning planets of the universe—all merged into an illogical resplendence that was quite addictive. I could easily get my 'fix' by chanting some memorised lines and pronouncing the special q, z, gh and kh sounds of Urdu with dramatic exaggeration. Even though the meaning of what I recited was a mystery to me, I could summon up the atmosphere. My friends envied the access they thought I had to the glamorous world of Urdu poetry. Akhtari Bai Faizabadi as she was known then was the authentic symbol of this world and her voice was the most effective magic wand there could be for me.

Many genres of Indian singing entail softening or modulating the voice in an effort to create delicacy and beauty but this was not her way at all. She seemed to collect herself like an archer taking aim, and hit each note dead centre with great energy, allowing the surplus charge of sound to spill over naturally. She was genetically so tuneful, so *sureela,* that the directness and honesty of her voice-throw sometimes resulted in a characteristic break (or *patti*), in her voice which 'killed' connoisseurs and was hailed by listeners as an inimitable core of beauty in her music. Her audiences always waited for such euphoric moments in each recital and greeted them with sighs of rapture. She never tried to produce this effect. It happened spontaneously, almost absent-mindedly, but the effect was electrifying. The impact of her voice on the note produced sparks, as when flint stones are rubbed together. Her famous patti became the envy of all her contemporaries and as a ghazal singer she had no equal. Even her rivals had to concede this.

I loved her voice and needed no special education to react to it. But to understand the art of ghazal singing at its most evolved was another matter altogether. I never set out to learn the structure and dynamics of the couplet. But comprehension was forced upon me as a by-product of the simple and most enjoyable process of listening to Akhtari Bai with attention over a period of years. This also revealed to me some finer points of her craft, notably the skill with which she could combine and balance music, words, and meaning in a single creative impulse.

Purists have a point when they say that music is articulate only in its own language and in no other. Pure music is not concerned with the meaning of the words that accompany, embellish or assist it in any fashion, however poetic or moving those words may be. And yet the harmonious co-existence of poetry and music runs through the fabric of the Indian tradition as exemplified by the bhakta saints, Sufis and folk singers. In these cases, music can owe a good deal of its poignance to the words it clothes but that does not change the fact that words and meaning are extraneous to music. The ghazal too is a self-sufficient literary form with an integrity of its own. If it has vitality and enduring value it should need no aids or props from the world of music.

The greatness of poets like Mir, Momin, and Ghalib owes nothing whatsoever to music. In fact originally the ghazal, which literally means 'addressing the beloved', was never meant to be sung or set to music. The practice of reciting in *tarannum* is still frowned upon by orthodox literary connoisseurs because the intrusion of melody, which sneaks in with a small demand of its own, blurs the word structure and disturbs the natural flow of the line. Akhtari Bai sang the ghazal with such insight and sensitivity that she created a new area where poetry and music were simultaneously enhanced.

Her first principle was to leave the greatest poetry alone, so that her music would not flounder under its heavy weight. This principle was obviously and sensibly borrowed from the thumri form where the poetry of the text is suggestive and ambivalent by design so that the interpreter can choose freely from a multiplicity of possible meanings. Guided by this experience, Akhtari Bai usually picked lightweight ghazals that could be easily moulded to a musical purpose without damage to either. Her most popular ghazals, *Ai muhabbat tere anjaam pe rona aya*, and an earlier hit, *Deewana banana hai to deewana bana de*, are examples. Even when she chose to render verses of indifferent literary value, they leapt to instant fame while the bulk of the output of their authors sank into oblivion. Aspiring poets vied with each other to get an entry into her repertoire because that was a guarantee of recognition.

Another principle she adopted was from the genre of the khayal where the words of the composition exist mainly as sounds and not much as meaning. In her singing, the long vowels became flowing, graceful melodic arches while the hard consonants formed the pillars that supported them. She used the vast range of sounds offered by language, the liquid sounds, the sharp sibilants, the harsh gutturals, the nasal, throaty, or breathy consonants as musical raw material, and she did this with such amazing skill that the stoniest lines became delicious to the ear as in her rendering of Iqbal's *Kabhi ai haqeeqate muntazir nazar aa libaase majaaz men, Ke hazaaron sajde tadap rahe hain meri jabeene niyaaz men ...* The remarkable thing was that her musicality never lost track of the meaning of the poetry and her command over both was absolute.

Listening to her showed me what the structure of a typical couplet or *sher* of a ghazal was. Each is a self-contained unit in which the first line makes a non-committal statement which is not poetic or philosophic in itself. It only serves as a sort of background to the rules, as it were. The actual game begins only with the second line which retrospectively illuminates the introductory line and reveals the hidden meaning in a powerful backlash. There is a point at which the second line turns and looks over its shoulder at what has been said in the first line, suddenly suffusing it with a significance that was not apparent before this point. For instance, *Yoon to har sham umeedon men guzar jati thi* is the innocuous first line of an unremarkable couplet. It is just a setting of expectancy meant to highlight the flash of comprehension located in the second hemistich, *Aaj kuch baat hai jo sham pe rona aayaa*. As I recognised this pattern in verse after verse, I realised that I had been led to this understanding only by the cadences of Akhtari Bai's music. The low-key statement of the first line was set to music that in a way matched an introductory alaap. The music rose to a climax at the precise point at which the couplet turned to look back and shed light on the meaning of the whole sher. There was such a close correspondence between the ebb and flow of the music and the dynamics of the couplet that an understanding was almost thrust on me. No other ghazal singer can dance so gracefully, so closely with the poet.

Indeed, she became better and better at her art as she matured. The last ten years of her life represented a pinnacle that her earliest work had promised. My first recollection of her is a high-pitched voice, urgently announcing her name at the end of a ghazal sung on a 78 rpm disc brought out by HMV. 'Mera naam Akhtari Bai Faizabadi,' the voice proclaimed, abruptly cutting off the magic of the music and the glamour of the poetic Urdu words that had gone before. I was then not old enough to understand the relevance of this strange vocal signature. The grown-ups in my family who swooned over Akhtari Bai's music explained that many artistes who recorded in the decade between the 1920s and '30s followed this practice of shouting out their names at the end of each recorded item in the innocent belief that it would prevent their work from being plagiarised or pirated! I was as fascinated by this as by the music and played the discs again and again, fantasising that this famous singer, who was a living legend even then, was personally telling me her name. I could never have imagined that one day, forty years later, this would really happen, that she would actually speak to me and that we would become friends.

Much happened in these forty years. The attitude to music and musicians among families like mine became much more tolerant and receptive. Listening to music and even learning it were no longer frowned upon by 'respectable' families. On the contrary I felt that my love for music and my hero worship of personalities like Akhtari Bai were things my family began to be proud of. To my delight, all my moves in this direction were applauded. In these forty years Akhtari Bai also went through a metamorphosis. She had always been an extremely competent professional performer but over the years she matured into a creative musician who lavished extraordinary riches on the music world and contributed to it an irresistible manner and style which sent her listeners into ecstasy. She flowered into almost a cult figure, an ideal personality invested with such charm and charisma that an entire generation of women passionately wished to emulate her.

The impact of Begum Akhtar's music and personality on our generation is in many ways an inexplicable phenomenon. Many of her contemporaries were as gifted, as well-trained, and as much in command of their audiences as she was. Some were decidedly more hard working and unlike her did not spare themselves in the matter of discipline and practice. Many had larger repertoires and more extensive vocal ranges. Their singing styles were more elaborate and complicated than hers, and their musical material far more sophisticated. Yet her voice had a magic that nothing can explain and this special something had very little to do with musical skill or training.

The single most important quality that characterised her was effortlessness. She sang like a carefree bird, with no sign of strain on her features, her beautiful hands flowing like water over the keys of the harmonium. She smiled more with her eyes than her lips and despite her mercurial temperament, always carried herself with the utmost grace and dignity. Her contribution to our lives was a by-product of the full self-expression of an extraordinary personality, not something she consciously sought to achieve. One can say that she had no message to give but the way she lived, savouring to the fullest all that life had to offer, even if it was pain. She instinctively looked for beauty and refinement in all things and was truly upset each time they failed to appear. I remember an occasion when she was shocked by a music organiser of Delhi when he paid her her professional fee by thrusting a wad of notes into her hands, without even bothering to put it in an envelope.

She herself had so much polish in her manner that most things that happen in the music world seemed crude in comparison. *'Ishq se tabiyat ne, zeest ka mazaa paaya; dard ki dava paayi, darde-la-dava paaya.'* was one of her favourite couplets of Ghalib because she truly believed in the values set forth in it. The lines implied that the joy of living comes from the intensity of love, which is both an anodyne for pain and itself a pain without remedy. Akhtari Bai could not live without *ishq*, without being in love. If love did not happen, she had to invent it. And if the love she experienced was devoid of pain she had to invent the pain too. Only then could she feel alive. She lived each moment intensely, giving it all she could, but with great restraint and style. To my mind this temperament was responsible for her inimitable musical quality in which melancholy and sparkle were equal partners.

Akhtari Bai was born in 1914 to Mushtari Bai, a well-known professional singer of Faizabad. It was discovered quite early that this child had enough natural talent and charm to support herself if properly trained. Circumstances took her to Calcutta where her mother arranged for her to be trained in classical music by Ata Mohammad Khan of the Patiala gharana. She simply could not take the hard work that this rather dry style entailed and after a break in which she sang not khayal but ghazal, thumri and dadra, she tried again to learn the khayal gayaki from Ustad Abdul Waheed Khan, a pillar of the Kirana gharana. She was far too sensitive and intelligent not to have imbibed the basics of his invaluable training, but after a brief stint she discovered that khayal was not her forté. She never once sang khayal in public, though that was the only formal training she had received. She had grown up with the sound of music and the sweetness of Purabia, Avadhi, and Bhojpuri in her ears, so she evolved her own distinctive repertoire which captured the ethos and nostalgia of the culture of UP. To this fabric were added the rich nuances of Urdu poetry. Her music creates in the listener a yearning for a world of romance and dreams but at the same time imbues things of long ago and far away with the earthy flavour of the here and now. Her own personality underlines this synthesis, for she is both myth and fact. Hers is an utterance which is not only beautiful, but also faithful and true. It echoes the earthy sounds of the folk music of the Hindi belt as well as the sophistication of the princely courts which she frequented in the course of her career. The nawabs of Hyderabad, Bhopal, and Rampur and the maharaja of Kashmir employed her as a singer from time to time and treated her with special respect because of her dignified ways and the rare charm of her personality. Though she lived the life of a courtesan in the earlier part of her life, her natural bearing compelled the awe and deference usually reserved for royalty.

Despite the countrywide adulation she received, something in her hankered after a more settled and 'respectable' lifestyle, possibly because of its novelty, possibly because she got tired of dressing up for a new part in a new setting every day. With marriage as the goal, she set her sights on Ishtiaq Ahmad Abbasi, a talukdar of Kakori near Lucknow, and courted him in all seriousness. He was fond of music like all affluent members of his class at the time, but the main attraction of Akhtari for him was the novelty of the relationship and the fun it promised. He was a barrister-at-law educated in London. He sported a bow tie and rode to court in an old Chevrolet, but his attention was not on being a successful lawyer. Nor could his sprawling household of relatives ever have run on his professional earnings. When they got married, he happily basked in her glory and treated her like a great artist because the world told him that is what she was. In a sense he was her ultimate patron. She got a thrill from being a begum, as distinct from a bai. She relished the role of a devoted wife and used to polish her husband's shoes herself, as a matter of principle. For a while she willingly donned the shackles of life behind the purdah, and stopped singing altogether. But this could not last because music really was her life. At last Abbasi Sahib permitted her to perform again, provided it was outside the city of Lucknow.

An outstanding feature of Begum Akhtar's life was that she straddled two different worlds and wrested her identity as a woman from both without abandoning either of them. As a member of a puritanical Muslim family, she was never ashamed of being the *rasika* that she was. To her life was to be savoured and enjoyed, not just to be endured. She appreciated good taste and subtlety in all things—music, poetry, food, speech, dress—and was never ashamed of the little vanities that can bring pleasure to a woman's life. The poise and aplomb with which she lived her complicated life seems in the context of today the achievement of a pioneer and is bound to be valued by Indian women of our time who are asking penetrating questions about their entitlements. Her evolution as a human being is all the more remarkable considering the class and background she came from and the fact that she had hardly any formal education to speak of.

Begum Akhtar's music stands apart for its spontaniety and its fidelity to the classical idiom. Nothing she sings is a recipe worked out beforehand. For her musical communication itself is a creative act wherein she remains true to the reality of each moment. Never is hers a passive, premeditated recital. I remember an occasion when she was invited by All India Radio to sing four selected ghazals of Ghalib to celebrate the centenary of the poet in front of a live audience. I dropped in to see her in her hotel room just before the concert. She said casually to the small group of close associates who had come to escort her to the concert hall that she had decided on the ragas that would be suitable for the mood of each of the ghazals—Chayanat, Kedar, Darbari and Khammaj. There was a cry of approval from all present. However, when she began her recital only an hour later, her feeling had changed completely. She sang all four ghazals in Bhairavi, each different from the other and each outstanding! We were all dumbfounded. Her inexhaustible innovative skill could always be counted on to ensure that each musical moment was heartfelt and genuine. Her technique was also impressive. She leaned heavily on the khayal gayaki in which she had such excellent grounding and borrowed its stylised idiom and detachment even for light forms like thumri, dadra, kajri and chaiti. This lifted her utterance far above the merely personal and imbued it with the enduring, universal quality one associates with classical music.

EIGHT

Go, Lady, Go
Lady Linlithgow and the Taming of Raga Adana

No one who had seen Vinayak Rao bustling about the grounds of the music college in khaki shorts, knee-length stockings, and solar topi could possibly have imagined that he was the doyen of Hindustani classical music, an old-fashioned pandit at heart, an upholder of the performing traditions of the Gwalior gharana, and a nationally acclaimed figure in the music world. In the 1940s, an obsequious colonial culture still ailed government-aided institutions and his unlikely outfit that evening was perhaps an unconscious tribute to the Vicereine of India, Lady Linlithgow, who was expected on the premises at any moment. She was the chief patroness of the institution that employed him as a teacher of the khayal style of singing. In this case it only meant that her name was embossed in gold on their official stationery, even though all she had ever done for the institution was to lend it her weighty name, a gesture which presumably guaranteed that her imperial good wishes would be with them in all their cultural endeavours.

But now, the last Viceroy of India was leaving the country for good. It was only proper that his gracious lady, who had adorned the letterhead of the college for so many years, should be given a proper farewell. Arrangements for this very special occasion were under way. The principal had mobilised the entire staff to put their best foot forward. Vinayak Rao was supervising the seating and other mundane details in his khaki shorts, but his most important contribution to the musical evening planned for the dignitary was a khayal he had specially composed in her honour. His colleagues were intrigued and excited to hear this. But when they pressed him for details, he coyly said he would make the necessary announcement at the right time, that is, just before his performance.

The chief guest arrived punctually, escorted by Sir Ramaswami Mudaliar, an eminent member of the Viceroy's Executive Council. They were trailed by an assortment of aides and ladies-in-waiting. There was a sudden hush in the hall as the imposing procession approached the special upholstered seats in the front row. The only sound to be heard above the cautious whispers of the assembled gentry was the whirring of ancient ceiling fans and the authoritative tap-tap-tap of the high heels of Lady Linlithgow's splendid white court shoes on the cement floor. She wore matching elbow-length white gloves, a wide-brimmed summer hat decorated with bunches of violets, and a muslin tea gown in a print of overblown yellow roses. Her escort was almost equally resplendent in his compactly fashioned traditional turban of beige and gold cotton. He was on hand to receive and respond to any casual remark issuing from the lips of the honoured guest, and generally interpret the goings-on, which were still strange for her, despite her many years in India.

The proceedings began with orations and eulogies directed at 'our noble patroness' who had 'graced this occasion with her august presence'. Each member of the staff undertook this exercise in turn, displaying a wide variety of accents, styles and tonal pitches. Lady Linlithgow smiled and nodded her head ever so slightly in gracious acknowledgement, dabbing her beaded upper lip with a lace handkerchief. Then it was the turn of the B list. All participants, including electricians, caterers, casual helpers and guests were also thanked profusely for their various contributions in making the evening memorable. With all this out of the way, it was time for the *piece de resistance* to be unloosed on the audience.

Behind the curtain, Vinayak Rao was still in a dither, hissing last minute instructions about the refreshments to be served during the interval while his pupils tuned the instruments. It had slipped his mind that he was still in the working outfit he had donned while supervising arrangements earlier in the day. A senior colleague pointed out that he could not go on stage like that since no Indian raga could possibly be evoked in a solar topi. Then it all came back to him. Of course he had brought along his regular concert clothes in a bundle in the morning! He flung the offending head dress off and replaced it with a pugree. He covered his shirt with a long button-up coat of khadi silk. Half a dozen glittering medals awarded for extraordinary feats of musicianship at various times by various princely states were already affixed to the upper part of this garment as it was part of his special concert costume. A dhoti restored him to the image his audiences associated with him, but at the last minute he forgot to discard the thick sports stockings. A faithful pupil resourcefully flung a shawl over the master's feet as he settled down on the dais between two tanpuras.

It was clear that the music community was awaiting the promised announcement more eagerly than the chief guest who could have had no inkling of the trial in store for her. 'It is my proud privilege to present a khayal I have specially composed in honour of our gracious patroness', Vinayak Rao began in the approved eulogistic style of the day. 'It is in the festive and joyful raga Adana. The song is set to teentaal, a cycle of sixteen beats. The text celebrates the name of the noble Lady Linlithgow who reigns in our hearts this evening.'

In keeping with the prevailing custom, which had also been adopted by comperes of All India Radio, the eminent performer recited the opening words of the text of the khayal he proposed to sing. This practice normally served the double purpose of both setting the right mood for the impending recital and of identifying the opus for future reference if need be. However, in this case, the opening words were not exactly suggestive since they consisted only of the name of the distinguished personage sought to be honoured.

'The opening line of the khayal is Lay-dee Lin-litha-go', Vinayak Rao announced with folded hands. He then cleared his throat, nodded his approval of the tuning to the accompanists and started to sing.

The first word of the song was 'lady'. He pronounced it 'Lay Dee' and delivered it in two powerful notes, one for Lay and one for Dee, giving both syllables absolutely equal weight, as in a spondee, innocently defeating the word's original trochaic intent. A long and very pregnant pause separated the two syllables, presumably to heighten the dramatic effect of the climax of the sung line, or *sam*, when it occurred. This delectable moment at the end of each rhythm cycle is what lay listeners avidly wait for. The *sam* is as crucial as the punch line in a joke and has therefore to be tight and perfectly timed. In this recital, it coincided with the 'gow' of Linlithgow. The preceding syllables in the word, that is 'Linlith', had to function as a sort of musical run up to the *sam*, rather like the spurt of speed a bowler puts on before he actually pitches the ball at the wicket. With this kind of musical end in view, Vinayak Rao hurled the available syllables in the air, like a whiplash before it lands to punish the target. 'Lay-he-dee—li-hi-li-hi-tha—*go*', he sang in perfect rhythm to the beat of the tabla. The only trouble was that he had to drop the 'n' sound from the dignitary's name because it simply did not fit the metre. So the 'n' faded from the scene without so much as a murmur. Nor did the regular listeners miss it. Lady Linlithgow was obviously not one of them. In fact this was the first (and probably the last) time she had been subjected to such a performance. In any case, she had no idea that the singing had anything to do with her name. Any resemblance promised by the announcement had long since been obliterated by the energetic embellishments lavished on the music by Vinayak Rao.

'Lay-dee go, go *go*, lay-dee go, go, *go*, lay-dee go, go, *go*', went the passionate song. The singer intensified its burden by shifting the accent across the syllables in mind-boggling variations such as '*Lay*-di-go, lay-di-go, lay-*dee*-go, *lay*-dee-*go*, lay-dee *go*, go-o-o-o. ...' All Lady Linlithgow could make of this was that some mysterious musical compulsion caused the artist to emit an ear splitting 'go' at regular intervals. She was also convinced that the word 'go' was directed at her, because each time he sang it, he would open his eyes wide and stare at her meaningfully. This was supposed to be a farewell in her honour. In the circumstances, urging her to 'go' was hardly a civil way of expressing parting good wishes. She was genuinely puzzled, and wondered whether she should resort to the stiff upper lip or call for a clarification.

She opted for the latter. Turning to her escort she said with a characteristically British mixture of frost and wit, 'The gentleman seems overly insistent on our departure, considering that we are leaving shortly, anyway.' It took Sir Ramaswami a while to get her drift, since he was not too familiar with the local cultural and musical idiom either. But he gallantly resolved to find out what had been troubling her. He summoned one of the students in attendance and confided to him in a stage whisper that the singer's repeated stress on the word 'go' had given the chief guest the impression that she was being urged to leave, which was not very polite, to say the least.

Of course, this was a disastrous development. Nothing could have been further from the intentions of the institution. The student was terribly flustered and rushed backstage with his explosive information, which was relayed in several stages and dialects to the innocent perpetrator. The singing stopped for a moment while a staunch supporter explained the nature of the misunderstanding in broken Marathi. Vinayak Rao was unfazed. He had been nurtured by the sturdiest of classical traditions and had the resources to overcome any difficulty, musical or otherwise. 'I can settle this in no time, thanks to the training I have received from the gurus of the Gwalior gharana', he said confidently to the small group of devotees who had gathered on the stage around him in this hour of need. '*Bol baant* (word division and syllable-play) is a speciality of ours. You will all see for yourselves what I do now.'

The new motivation made the second phase of the concert more urgent and intense. As he had done the first time, Vinayak Rao threw the syllables

Lay and Dee into the air, as an invocation to the guest of honour. This time, even she recognised the direct address. But then, he suddenly switched the position of the component syllables. What accosted the ear sounded like an entreaty constructed with spondees. 'Lay-dee, Dee-lay, Dee-lay, Dee-lay, Lay-dee!' The surname was abandoned as a measure of caution, since it contained the explosive syllable 'go' and tended to spill out of the traditional beat. The revised version of the presentation repeatedly requested Lady Linlithgow to delay her departure. This was done in a dazzling display of metrical feet. '*Lay*-di, *Dee*-lay, *Lay*-di, *Dee*-lay, *Lay*-di, *Dee*-lay', he sang in perfect trochees, followed by iambs and spondees in a bewildering variety of permutations and combinations. Lay-*di*-di-*lay*, Lay-*di*-di-*lay*, Lay-*di*-di-*lay* formed an attractive triplet (*tihai*) which fitted neatly into the case provided by the versatile sixteen-beat cycle. Vinayak Rao's inventiveness was breathtaking. His consonants hopped, skipped, and collided as he subjected the words 'lady delay' to the full treatment, as though he had put the text in a food processor and was chopping it up in every possible shape and size.

The recital ended in triumph. With so much expenditure of energy, it could hardly have been otherwise. Lady Linlithgow may not have grasped the finer points of Vinayak Rao's singing style, but the message couched in his strenuous efforts was now crystal clear.

He did not really want her to go.

NINE

A Taste of British Guiana

Many years ago, my husband was posted to British Guiana. Abhinav, my four-year-old son was quite lost in the strange new environment. He did not yet know a single word of English and I was his only connection with life. He followed me around all day, clinging to the palla of my sari, unable to make any sense of the sights and sounds of the world to which he had been exiled. He demanded that I distract, reassure and comfort him all his waking hours, in addition to interpreting everything new he encountered. I could not free myself for the very urgent business of setting up house unless I deposited him in a school. My husband was certainly not going to share any baby-sitting with me. He was completely immersed in his UN assignment and quite understandably expected me to deal with everything else in our lives.

I heroically decided to deposit Abhinav in school and face the necessary traumas as they came up. The Convent of the Good Shepherd was recommended by casual neighbours. I immediately presented myself and my unwilling offspring to Mrs. Ambler, an earnest British missionary who was the head of the nursery section there. I explained the situation and the language problem. She was most helpful and admitted him right away. He was finally led away to his class kicking and screaming, unmoved by the soothing, cooing sounds Mrs. Ambler directed at his reluctant ears. I left with a heavy heart but a feeling of freedom.

Abhinav had to be driven to his place of execution every day and abandoned for several hours before he was rescued. The first month of school was nerve-racking for all concerned. But what happened next can only be described as a gradual miracle. He began to speak the sing-song patois of the street with ease and increasing enthusiasm. The Hindi he knew disappeared without trace.

'Dat boy, he comin down the street an hittin me, maan. So I hittin he back,' he told me one day. The accent, intonation and local liberties with grammar made this variety of English an intimate and warm tool of communication. The dramatic, all pervasive present tense and the innocent linguistic economies charmed me. More than that, I was relieved that Abhinav would at last be able to crawl out of his isolation into a more normal life.

He grew more and more confident with his newfound language and began to use it even to communicate with me. 'My teacher, she stoopaid!' he declared one day. I tried to hush him, lazily explaining that one did not say things like that about one's teachers. The remark popped up again a few days later. 'Miz Ambler, she stoopaid, I tellin yo, Ma.' When it became a regular refrain in the next few weeks, I decided to probe.

'Why do you think that?' I asked.

'Every day she aksin me hello whats yoh name an I tellin she my name be Abnow, but she still aksin and aksin hello whats yoh name!'

This was not enlightening. Nor did the song die down on its own as I had hoped. I was a neurotic mother trying to bring up my first-born according to Dr. Spock's classic textbook and therefore morbidly believed that my son's unfamiliar name in this alien setting must have made him a butt of ridicule in school. Undoubtedly Dr. Spock's view would be that an awareness of being somehow different from his peers would damage my child psychologically. The thought scared me. There was no choice but to call on the good Mrs. Ambler with all the tact I was capable of. I dragged Abhinav along as a sort of key witness in the case.

Obviously I couldn't tell her exactly what my son had been saying again and again about her being stupid. But I produced an edited version which might serve the same purpose without being offensive.

'Abhinav feels you are having some difficulty with his name,' I stuttered. 'If that is so, we could simplify it. We sometimes call him Abe at home ...'

She was frankly puzzled.

'Oh no, not at all. I know the name of each child in my class very well. I make it a point. There is no problem at all. Your son's name is A-B-H-I-N-A-V, is it not?' she said, slowly spelling it out for me, and pronouncing it with startling clarity.

She gazed expectantly at me. I had no idea what to say next. There was an uncomfortable lull in which I looked at the floor and Abhinav fidgeted maddeningly.

'What does the child actually say to you?' she asked in a clear voice, peering at us through gold-rimmed glasses.

'Well, he seems to think you say hello to him everyday when you ask him his name ...'

'Hello? That is extraordinary indeed! Umm. Let us see what this could possibly be.'

She turned the word around in her mind like a detective who has scented a clue. After a moment, her penny dropped. She put her hand on her forehead and allowed herself a girlish titter.

'It's the Lord's Prayer he is talking about! Well, I never! You see the class is expected to repeat the prayer after me every morning. Each child is able to say Our Father who art in Heaven, Hallowed be thy Name. Everyone except Abhinav to whom the words still mean nothing. So he just stands there. When I prompt him, the only response I get is "My name be Abno"!'

The mystery was cleared. Poor Abhinav's recent linguistic achievements could not possibly include words like 'Hallowed'. Both Mrs. Ambler and I reconstructed the scene in our minds. During the scripture class, Mrs Ambler would fix her eye on him and say encouragingly 'Hallowed be thy Name', trying to guide him to speak the line along with the others. What he got from this daily exercise was that Mrs Ambler had made a routine of saying 'Hello, what's your name,' despite his telling her his name every day. And so he had come to his own conclusion about her mental capability.

Ours was the last house on Campbell Street in Georgetown. Beyond this freshly painted new structure, all human habitation unbelievably came to an abrupt end. There were a couple of uneven but lush green lots, covered with weeds and hyacinth and then a stretch of inky water almost wholly covered with bright pink water lilies. Looking at this from my living room window, I had the sensation that this indeed must be the end of the earth. Lotus bloomed on the dark water as far as I could see. I was sure that beyond that there could only be nothingness. To my dusty Indian eyes, the colours of everything I saw here were so vivid as to be almost startling. The stars at night were bigger and brighter and the sky an unreal, picture-book blue I had never seen anywhere before. But the Guianese people in the streets, in contrast to their vibrant setting, seemed mild and lackadaisical at first sight. The population was very mixed and I was soon able to distinguish the natives from those who did not really belong. The outsiders were conspicuous because of their higher energy levels and the air of earnestness and anxiety they wore, probably because like me they were in Georgetown for a purpose and had to justify their presence within a defined period.

When we had landed at Atkinson Field airport a couple of months earlier, I had experienced another kind of unreality. I could hardly believe my eyes when I saw a prominently displayed sign that read 'No Singing Allowed.' This was not a mistake as I first thought. The entire building was dotted with the same announcement, in different colours and type sizes. Very intriguing, I thought. But it began to make sense as soon as we took our place at the tail end of a queue. The man ahead of us had a guitar strapped to his waist and started to strum softly, obviously to pass the time while he was waiting his turn. He compulsively moved his hips and shoulders in time to the music in his mind, while his lips soundlessly shaped the words of the song he was obviously itching to sing. This harmless movement triggered off a shot of energy that ran through the length of the queue, and in no time at all electrified everybody, or rather all those who were Guianese or Trinidadian. They all slowly began to sway, tap, gyrate and undulate in response to the irresistible call of the guitar. The prime mover had started tentatively, chanting the words of a calypso under his breath, but it gradually became a full-blooded song and all those who could, joined in. All official business forgotten, the queue broke up and smoothly turned into a joyful revel. 'Dee bard and dee pijon, Were quite good compaanion', they all sang ecstatically. The official at the window, obviously a local person, pushed his papers aside and looked rapturously on, longing to be a part of the festivities. One frantic outsider repeatedly asked the time of departure of a flight to Chicago but failed to get the official's ear. When he persisted, the official sleepily dislodged an aged schedule from a shelf with the help of a cane, releasing clouds of dust, and murmured reassuringly, 'Afther launch, afther launch, dez right, no hurry!'

I subsequently found that this introduction to the Caribbean temperament was quite faithful. Every day provided some fresh evidence of the people's talent for happiness and their commitment to whatever kind of good life circumstances allowed. I once saw a gathering that started out as a funeral but turned imperceptibly into a rollicking party, just on the strength of human company and liquor. So long as these were assured, it was not unusual for those present to disregard what had brought them there in the first place. This could on occasion also be true of public places of business. After a while, I began to understand the 'No Singing' signs I had seen at the airport.

However, the Guianese of Indian origin seemed to be somewhat different. They were notorious for being focused and hard-working. It was said that even at the time of the Carnival, they hardly lifted their heads from the soil they were tilling on both sides of the road, unaffected by the loud music and the boisterousness of the parades as they went by. They clung to their Indian identity and took great pride in their customs and festivals.

I had made friends with a tomato seller called Buddhoo who used to go from house to house on a bicycle, dressed in a brown felt hat and Bermuda shorts.

'Tammara is Janamashtami Ma'am. Will you come to the Hindoo church?' he said one day.

This I was not going to miss for anything. The next evening I dragged my husband to the address Buddhoo had given and for the first time entered a 'Hindoo church'. Nothing could have been less like a noisy Indian temple during Janamashtami. This was a large, white wooden structure with a church-like dome and balustrades. Inside there was awed silence though the space was crowded with people. Men and women sat in separate sections in the pews, humble and expectant. Soon a 'priestess' appeared and made her way down the aisle to the altar. Her head was covered with an *orhni* that could have come from any village of eastern UP, but she wore high-heeled shoes and a knee-length Western-style dress. She gave some kind of signal in a dialect I did not understand, and the women, dressed in the same combination of East and West, rose one by one, each with a *thali* carrying the familiar offering of coconut, banana, red paste, flowers and a lighted oil lamp. The priestess accepted the thalis on behalf of the divine from each devotee in turn. It was a disciplined ritual, without any scrambling or raised voices.

There was a sudden ripple of excitement. 'De paandhit-jee comin, de paandhit-jee comin', someone exclaimed loudly, as an elderly car rattled to a stop outside the entrance and an extraordinary personage alighted. A wide brimmed straw hat which seemed several sizes too large for him topped his grave, weather-beaten face. He wore knee-high gumboots and sported a long, flowing nylon scarf in place of an *angavastram*. His body language suggested that he should have had a long white beard like Moses or Abraham, although in fact the growth on his face was only one day old as far as I could judge. With the air of a royal personage, he moved importantly to the altar, looking imperiously left and right. Everyone including the priestess froze in deference.

The self-appointed master of ceremonies who had excitedly announced the arrival of the panditji now took up another refrain. 'He comin for de ser-mon, he comin for de ser-mon!' The word was pronounced in two separate parts, the first half in a descending tone where the lowest point was held for an instant before the 'mon' part of the word was released as though by a little catapult to ascend to the normal pitch of the voice. The word when pronounced in Guianese style sounded like a caress.

The panditji mounted the pulpit and cleared his throat. There was no microphone and I knew we were in for a spell of serious bellowing.

'Today bein Jan-am-ash-tamee, I tellin ya bout Gita, wat Krishna tellin de whole world. Wat he tellin Arjuna on de baatle-field of Kurukshetra, dat he tellin you and dat he tellin me!' Panditji roared in the manner of a prophet of the Old Testament, his imaginary white beard flowing in the wind.

The audience was rivetted and suitably intimidated, since the manner of the address suggested that doomsday could not be far.

'Wat Krishna tellin Arjuna on de baatlefield of Kurukshetra? Well, wat he tellin Arjuna, dat he tellin you dat and dat he tellin me. Is Krishna tellin Arjuna "Doan be eatin, doan be drinkin, doan be dancin?" No, no, no. He not tellin Arjuna dat, he not tellin you dat, he not tellin me dat.'

Panditji paused for effect, at which point my husband whose ear was not his strong point whispered: 'What language is he speaking? I think it's a garbled version of Sanskrit.'

He was incredulous when I said it was more likely to be a version of English.

The local prophet had warmed up and was now in full cry, repeating his theme in bhajan style.

'Is Krishna sayin to Arjuna "doan be drinkin, doan be dancin, doan be makin love, doan be enjoyin?" No, no, no! He not tellin Arjuna dat, he not tellin you dat, and he not tellin me dat! He sayin "enjoy all—food, drink, dancin, makin love!"'

The rhetoric took on a menacing tone as he shook his fist at the cowering congregation.

'Yea, be eatin, drinkin, dancin, makin love!' he thundered. 'Only remember, this all belongin to Krishna and HE GONNA TAKE BAACK WHEN TIME KOM!'

You could have heard a pin drop in the Hindoo church. Doomsday was at hand.

We went home in silence, carrying with us forever the most original interpretation of the Gita ever offered by mankind.

TEN

The Many-Splendoured Harmonium

I could never have believed that at the ripe age of fifty-five, I would fall in love with the tone of a harmonium! I had considered the instrument an abomination throughout my life and was not at all prepared for what happened to me one wet evening at the Alternative Museum in New York. My life had suddenly cut me off from Indian music and I was so starved for it that anything that could even remotely remind me of my lost world was welcome. I saw in the newspapers that a Baul singer was to perform at this small centre for experimental art. Even though this was not my kind of music, I hungrily made my way to the address given in the New York Times in the hope that I would at least hear some healing sounds.

It was impossible for anyone or anything to be unobtrusive in the space to which I was led by unconventional ushers. Everyone present was an original, in their own fiercely individual way. Funky music addicts with blue-dyed hair, clean-shaven Buddhist monks of European extraction, nostalgic Asians like myself, and regular, curious metropolitan young people interested in 'happenings' mingled self-consciously with one another as they found places to sit, squat or perch. The walls were plastered with the lurid art of over-confident young rebels which the organisation obviously supported. I could not help thinking that it would be difficult to have traditional Indian concerts here, because the paintings were of the screaming variety and would have clashed hopelessly with the mood of almost any raga I could think of. The room was thick with human vibrations and I wondered with motherly concern how the simple Baul singer from Bangladesh would fare.

I need not have worried. The Baul was quite at home. In fact he seemed to be carrying his home with him in his mind and confidently expected his audience to share it. The first plaintive cry of his hoarse voice was so convincing that everyone was transported. The instruments followed suit. The ill-tuned drums began to rumble happily, and the strings twanged and rasped to a compulsive rhythm. It was hypnotic but disturbingly off-key. I consoled myself with the thought that at least the atmosphere was close to what I was longing for, even though there was nothing to soothe my ear.

Just then, a dishevelled member of the Baul's party returned from the wash room, smiled uncertainly, and casually took his place behind a waiting harmonium. He ran his cadaverous fingers over the keys to test the instrument. The melody that emerged took my breath away. It was the most tuneful, beautiful sound I had heard for months. Certainly I had never come across a harmonium that could hold its own like this. The double reeds were perfectly tuned, the tone was like velvet, and the silent breath had incredible range. Undoubtedly the creation of a master craftsman, I thought. The relief from the earlier sounds was overwhelming. I was so grateful to the wielder of this magic box that I rushed to congratulate him at the end of the evening. I was also curious about the instrument-maker whose skill had given me so much unexpected pleasure, but to my amazement the player seemed quite unaware of the quality of what he had just played. 'The *baja* is not ours. We have borrowed it from him', he said pointing to a slightly flabby, clean-shaven man in his early forties. Owning and cherishing an instrument like this had so many implications that I just had to meet the real owner. He was bound to be an extraordinary musical person, exactly the kind of friend I needed just then. I asked to be led to him forthwith.

When I was facing him, I introduced myself, first in English, and then, encouraged by his polite and authentic '*ji*', I slipped comfortably into

Hindustani. He was much younger than I was, and was deferential in a way I had become unused to. He was not articulate in English but the *Dilli ka muhavara* I deliberately served up to him evoked a powerful response. He was also from the old city of Delhi but had not spoken or heard good Urdu for twenty years. For ten years he had lived among Punjabis in Lahore, and then had escaped to the USA to settle down in Queens in the state of New York. He was yearning for a cultural reconnection with his roots. He told me his name was Shahid Akhtar Khan and we were soon chatting like long-lost friends. He glowed and blushed when I complimented him on his wonderful harmonium. 'Yes, it is in great demand in the Tri-state area,' he said with that special mixture of modesty and pride that only people from our subcontinent know how to use. The Baul party had returned the harmonium to him by now and it rested on a nearby chair draped in a laced dark green velvet cover that looked a hundred years old. He stroked and patted it lovingly as though it was a prize racehorse.

Now it was time for him to say something nice to me. Civilities snowballed as they often do in oriental settings. Shahid complimented me on my speaking voice and my accent which reminded him of his mother, his favourite aunt, the *mohalla* of Ballimaran that he had grown up in, and everything else that was dear to him. Would I please go on talking to him in Urdu? Would I also please agree to talk to his elder sister on the telephone? She would be very grateful. She was married to a Polish businessman and lived in a state of pathological homesickness in New Jersey with no relief in sight. I asked Shahid whether he himself was a musician. No, he said, though he adored music. I gathered in slow stages that his area of activity was as far from music as it could possibly be. He worked as a loader with Pakistan International Airways at Kennedy Airport. This I was not prepared for.

The life injections by telephone became a daily occurrence after this encounter, a sort of game. Sometimes the homesick sister would also participate. We would all deliberately try to speak a formal, flowery, overly polite, almost courtly Urdu of long ago that could not possibly have meant anything in our frenetic New York existence. Shahid was going to be my humble servant for ever. The opportunity to be of use to an incomparable artist like myself was his great good fortune and he would pray to the Almighty that the privilege should never be denied him. He had decided that I was a great musician without ever having heard me perform. I protested, but he just knew because this was something God had told him personally. He clinched the argument by saying I was like his mother and the Holy Book said that heaven lay under the mother's feet. I countered his avalanches repeatedly by equally stately rejoinders. I was not worthy of such devotion. I had done nothing to deserve it. God had shown me His mercy by leading me to Shahid through his harmonium. And so on. Anyhow, we got mildly addicted to this sort of exchange and began to use it as an intoxicant fairly regularly. Meanwhile both Shahid and I continued to toil at our respective roles in the city of New York, both more secure in the knowledge that a reliable new supporter was now only a phonecall away.

When the ardour of our first exchanges subsided a little, I asked Shahid how he had acquired his harmonium. It could not have too many peers. I had once seen something like it in Lucknow in the possession of Begum Akhtar. I remembered her telling me that she had personally supervised every stage of its construction and assembly with a famous craftsman of Calcutta, and that it had taken two years to complete and another three for its tone to 'take on colour'. I knew that Shahid himself could not have had the resources or ability to make the same kind of effort. He told me frankly that the instrument belonged to Farida Khanum, a celebrated ghazal singer of Pakistan, who was the mother-in-law of a friend of his who also lived in Queens. She had not been able to carry it back with her after a concert tour in the States and had left it in the indefinite custody of her son-in-law to be transported at a future date. Meanwhile, the son-in-law had been transferred to Atlanta, Georgia, and had left his clutter with his friend. Ten years had passed and nobody seemed to be doing anything about restoring the harmonium to its owner. So far as Shahid was concerned it was like a stray cat who had sneaked into his house and decided to live with him. The harmonium was his by default. Even though he was not directly aware of its virtues, its performance as a magic carpet that could fly him almost anywhere slowly convinced him that he had come by a treasure.

I had known Shahid for about two months when I got my first chance to perform in New York city. A wealthy American patron of Indian dance and music organised an evening for interested people in his large apartment in Manhattan and invited me to give a vocal recital. I accepted at once and excitedly rang up Shahid. At last I could be on stage along with his fabulous harmonium! Would he accompany me? Yes, yes, of course, there was no question! He would go with me to the ends of the earth! He would take leave from his job, stand on his head, do whatever was needed. It would be an unprecedented honour for him, this worthless *nacheez*, to be associated with my wonderful music. Clearly, it was all settled.

On the appointed evening, he came to our apartment in a flashy maroon car to take me and my large tanpura to the scene of action. He was dressed in an impressive Pakistani salwar suit and smelt of musk or something equally overpowering. When I introduced him to my husband and elder son, he was courtesy itself. But my family wasn't quite sure how to react, specially since I could not tell them where we were going and for how long. Shahid was taking care of the details and I was quite happy to be in his hands. 'If you are not back by midnight, I'm going to the police', my son stage-whispered fiercely as we left.

The fashionable Fifth Avenue apartment which was our destination had been turned into a *baithak* fit for an Indian cultural evening. *Diyas* flickered in antique brass lamps. Most of the American guests were turned out in ethnic Indian fabrics, beads and chunky silver jewellery which proclaimed their interest and support. An Indian dancer who lived in New York had brought a huge bowl of kheer 'for afterwards' and smilingly garnished it with red rose petals as she set it on the table meant for refreshments. Shahid and I settled down decorously on the Irani carpet with our instruments.

Someone quickly checked the sound system and the recording apparatus. I gave the final touches to the tuning of my tanpura. Shahid unveiled the harmonium and rested his fingers on the keys. His eyes were fixed expectantly on my face. At last the moment had come.

I started by singing a long note to introduce the raga. Even before I could hear myself properly, Shahid burst into a volley of applause. '*Wah, wah! Kya kehne! Kya baat hai, kya awaaz hai!*' he expostulated, startling and mystifying everyone including me. Two things were clear. One, that he had no ear for music; otherwise he would have waited till I had really done something with my voice before exploding like that. Second, his enthusiasm had no connection with my calibre as a singer. He was determined to lionise me for some complicated psycho-cultural reasons of his own that I could not quite fathom. I was nonplussed but plodded on with the recital. At this point I noticed that no sound was emerging from the harmonium although Shahid was constantly emitting sounds of appreciation for my efforts from his throat. He concentrated his attention on the smallest whisper I might produce but his fingers lay inert on the keys. I gestured to him several times to begin playing but absolutely nothing happened. He did not even know what to do with the bellows. He gestured back helplessly, and to my utter disbelief mouthed the words 'I don't know how to *play*', as though this was just a minor detail.

To Shahid, the harmonium was an important object in a serious ritual and he was the designated attendant. He saw nothing incongruous in the situation. Even while I was singing, it came to me in a flash that to him it was not so much a musical instrument as an insurance against loneliness. Because of it, he was in great demand too and on its wings was regularly able to escape from the dreariness of his suburban American existence. For him it was a credit card, an entrance ticket to a warmer and more friendly world, a priceless possession which lent him value and eminence. I thought of the accident which had left the harmonium in his care. A strange sympathy for him and his utter ignorance of the ways of the music world welled up in me. However, this did not faze him in the least and he continued to greet the smallest musical phrase I uttered with loud cries of appreciation and encouragement, like a fervent spectator at a bull fight. There was no way out of my embarrassment. I could hardly pretend that I had nothing to do with him. We were clearly a duo, joined at the waist so far as the audience was concerned and the sum total of the sound input this evening was squarely my responsibility.

At last my ordeal ended and the host invited the guests to ask any questions they wished. There were a number of innocuous ones which were neither here nor there. But then came a question that profoundly affected my own understanding of the music I had been practising for years. An earnest American lady from the Asia Society furrowed her brow with concentration and said in slow, measured tones that she wanted a clarification. 'The gentleman sitting to your left seemed to be saying a *lot* of things all through the concert. I want to know what that was. Was it a part of the song? Or the music? I must say the gentleman's constant participation didn't sound much like music but it seemed to fit right in!'

Nothing could have been more true. It set me thinking about some fundamental things. Yes, it was a part of the music in an organic sense, an inalienable part without which the intended communication in Indian music cannot really happen. Neither Shahid nor the lady from the Asia Society can have any idea how many doors they accidentally opened for my mind that evening.

ELEVEN

The New Face of Listening

Here I am. Now do something to please me, the eager young eyes seem to say, as their owner fussily subsides in the seventh row, a little to the left, better view, you see, and the best seats, sound-wise. It's a sort of party, so there are three others in tow. Two of them have to go out to dinner later; so they hope, very loudly, that the maestro will do his stuff fast, because they simply must leave by eight-thirty. The serious young man in jeans and khadi kurta carries a paperback, a battered Walkman, and an assortment of cassette tapes in a cloth sling bag, his arrangements for alternative activity just in case the evening doesn't work out.

The performer squints at the footlights and begins to tune up, to prepare psychologically for the ineffable and intimate disclosures that his art is all about. But his audience is no one in particular, just a vast black pit with an unknown animal in it. It might roar or pounce, purr or go to sleep. He has no way of knowing until he is more than halfway through. As he tries to concentrate and establish the first note, there is a hum of rival sounds.

'I think eight-thirty is cutting it too fine, yaar.'
'Don't fuss. It'll be o.k.'
'Look who's here ! Haaaiii! Didn't see you yesterday.'
'Couldn't make it. Was the music good?'

'Faantaastic! There were gorgeous guzzles at the end. I don't understand all the words, but Oordu is such a beautiful language ! I just love guzzles.'

'My God, what a smashing outfit! Where do you find such things?'

'Shhh. He's started, I think.'

'Will he do guzzles?'

'Don't be idiotic, yaar. He's dhurpad or something. Really heavy stuff! Now be quiet, for heaven's sake. I've heard he's really cool.'

When the music finally ends, there is uproarious clapping by eight hundred people, a shattering sound without tone or rhythm, a frightening cacophony that can immediately erase the beauty and meaning of what has gone before.

This, more or less, describes the new elements that have entered the scene at public concerts of classical music in any big city in India today. The atmosphere of the music world was fundamentally different only fifty years ago, which is why people of my generation tend to begin every sentence with the tiresome 'When we were young ...'

For one thing, the perception of silence is now quite different from what it has always been in the past. The century we have just entered is the noisiest one the world has ever known and India is no exception. Connoisseurs of the old school here used to regard silence as the starting point of all music. The portrait of a raga was thought to consist of unbroken melodic lines drawn on the canvas of silence. All traditional Indian music makes use of silence in many other subtle and delicate ways which are all but lost to the musician of today and of course, very sadly, to the listener as well. The gradual erosion of silence by ever-increasing noise levels is to my mind the single most important change that has come about in the music world in the last fifty years. It has irreversibly affected performers and coarsened listeners, producers, presenters and marketeers of music.

If one were to consider just the physical aspect of the music that is being produced today, one could justifiably say that it is louder and much more strident than it has ever been. This stems from the attitudes of both music maker and listener. Both have changed drastically in recent years. Music can no longer be the intimate communication that was its original intention. Now it has to be shouted out, not whispered, if it is to be heard at all above the din that pervades life today. To get and hold the attention of the listener, musicians can no longer depend entirely on their art. They have to make a little go a long way and too often have to resort to grandstanding and gimmicks.

The advent of the microphone has ushered in another major change. Along with other electronic aids and the mass media, it has extended the reach of both musician and listener. Of course methods of transmission must change if much larger audiences have to be reached, but must the product itself? Although this could not have been the intention, many examples spring to mind where the need to channel music through the microphone has killed many born singers and created several who would otherwise have been only hummers and crooners. The microphone is the new tyrant of the music world. It demands a kind of modulation which is alien to the direct and intimate idiom of Indian music. Not only that. By offering artificially an unaccustomed range of tonal possibilities, it often becomes an invitation to spurious emoting, posturing and striving after sound effects, specially for vocalists.

The saving grace for instrumentalists is that many of them are learning to use the potential provided by electronic amplification in a positive manner. In this they are guided by the extraordinary technological improvements that have taken place in almost all Indian instruments over the last fifty years. It is thrilling to hear clearly the echoes of the softest whisper of a string even after it has stopped vibrating. This was not the case in the instrumental music of even the greatest masters of the 1940s and 1950s. The vast expanse of musical space that audio technology has opened up offers to the creative musician limitless opportunities for experimentation. Many have used it with discrimination, and succeeded in introducing a new sophistication and refinement in the body of the old music. In irresponsible and casual hands however the danger of derailment is also immeasurably greater than it was before. Examples of this are also plentiful. In other words, the microphone like the curate's egg has turned out to be good in parts.

Correspondingly, the audience of today does not consist of connoisseurs who were brought up to tune in to the mind of the performing musician, but of a vigorous new class of passive listeners who feel entitled to the best that life has to offer and expect it to be served to them without any effort on their part. Today's patrons of music are more powerful than they have ever been in the history of Indian music. Their strength is in their numbers, in their omnipresence, their mobility, their boundless energy, and above all their determination to get the best there is. And access to the best has never been easier. The greatest music can quite affordably be in the hands of anyone who cares to buy a recorded cassette. One can listen at leisure, whenever and wherever one wishes. It has often occurred to me that at least physically every literate music lover can have almost as much in the way of music as the emperor Akbar might have had at the height of his power, and more. A myriad music events take place almost every day, at least in the big cities. Most of them are open to the public and charge no entrance fee, as they are usually sponsored by corporate enterprises engaged in building a more attractive image of themselves. Music and dance schools have sprung up almost at every street corner and it is altogether a most lucrative proposition for institutions to engage in all forms of cultural promotion.

Most serious listening in the not so remote past happened within the traditional *baithak*. Its hushed air of intelligent expectancy was an ideal setting for the delicate and intimate idiom of classical music. Each of the two-hundred-odd in the audience was aware of his or her role as a listener and had their responses finely turned to the extraordinary communication they were about to receive and be a part of, as ready to hear as the musician was to play or sing. The ideal for both was to share each phase of the creative process, to travel together to magic worlds which the musician had seen and was now about to share with admirers anxious to follow him. A performance was an intensely personal affair, with deeply entrenched rules of etiquette which spoke of a real cultural connection with the music. Only peers or elders could be vocal in their appreciation. Successful performances did not end with mechanical bursts of clapping, but human sounds such as *wah, wah! bahut khoob, kya kehne,* and so on. Younger enthusiasts had to hold themselves in. For them to express praise was considered presumptuous, even insolent. To fidget or change your posture while the baithak was in session was the height of bad manners. Eating, drinking or smoking during the music was taboo except in some degenerate courtly settings. Accompanists who tried to outshine the main performer were frowned upon and considered uncivilised. Of course one always removed one's footwear, but one could never stretch one's legs and point them in the direction of the instruments, as invariably happens today in soirees that claim to simulate the traditional setting. In short, in the old days one entered the presence of music with respect and humility. The musician was not someone who had been paid to deliver something to which the listener was entitled, but a living treasure to be cherished for what he was—a superior being. He was the leader and the listener the follower.

These roles have gradually been reversed because the musician must now please his new, many-headed patrons if he is to survive professionally. His stature no longer depends only on artistic merit. He has also to woo the big stage and cultivate a winning personality which is in keeping with the public's image of the sensitive artist. He must seem to be a superstar even if he has not yet made it. He must also learn to speak the language of organisers and promoters in addition to the wordless language of music. And most importantly, he must make sure that he sells. These are some of the pressures on the musician of today which his predecessors did not have to grapple with.

Electronic aids and the mass media have extended the reach of both the musician and the listener. That the new audiences are now at least a hundred times larger and consist mostly of the rising middle classes and young people in their twenties is undoubtedly a good sign from a social point of view. The treasures that our music has to offer are no longer the preserve of the privileged few. Music is for everyone. It is a commodity that is consumed like any other product in a fast changing society. This is a sign of development and must be welcomed. But something fundamental, and I suspect valuable, has been lost as a result. Inevitably the targets, the volume and the methods of transmission must change with progress. But must the product itself?

The germ of the big change has entered the very substance of music and laid a cold finger on its ancient values of restraint and purity. The intimacy of communication which was its life now too often gives place to unsubtle posturing and stagey oratorical styles which are quite alien to its original intention. The audiences of today, far from trying to refine their ear, confidently lay down their demands very explicitly through patterns of response. They want something 'that comes straight from the heart' but are oblivious that they might have a role to play in this exchange. To prove his worth the musician has to function alone. He must hold their attention and impress them somehow. Gimmicks, displays of virtuosity and spurious emoting are increasingly becoming the norm. This amounts to a passive dilution and vulgarisation, a lowering of quality in order to meet the expectations of the mass audience and stay in business. The challenge to the creativity of today's performing maestro is gigantic. He must innovate genuinely and so vigorously that the frontiers of his art stretch to admit the energetic audiences of the new commercial culture. Classical music might then become the most worthwhile, most consumable music even for the new audiences.

The motivations of the public that flocks to concert halls are also more varied than they have ever been. Not everyone who makes the effort to attend is necessarily interested in the music as used to be the case not so long ago. Many of the young come because they are in search of their lost cultural identity. Jaded politicians come to prop up their image. Socialites come to be seen and because it is a pleasant and possibly rewarding way to pass the time. Snobbery, curiosity, boredom, networking and entertainment are some other reasons which draw audiences and can sometimes account

THE NEW FACE OF LISTENING

for nearly half their number. This also confirms that after Independence, Indian music has gained immeasurably in prestige if not in genuine sources of artistic stimulus.

The ease with which the doors of the music world can now open has naturally brought in an element of casualness even among rising young musicians who seriously wish to excel. The intense devotion and dedication that used to be an inalienable part of the music business have rapidly waned although the level of activity on the music scene has risen to a feverish pitch. The sheer volume of the music that has to be produced to keep up with the demands also contributes to the dilution of quality. So does the rise of the personality cult. The average musician today would rather work at being a superstar than at deepening the material he has inherited or acquired. The press and television often publicise the appearance of a new raga specially crafted for this or that national occasion by some celebrity, while many rare and beautiful ragas that have existed for centuries languish and face extinction from sheer neglect. Most musicians are too busy 'doing' music in some form or other to ever think about it. No one considers *chintan* and *manan* a part of a musician's normal discipline, least of all the performing artists themselves. This is not how it used to be.

Another conspicuous change from the 1950s and 1960s is the loss of innocence among the practitioners of the art of music. Though the masters we admired in our youth were human and undoubtedly indulged their prejudices and jealousies, their art was the centre of their universe, in the same way in which a child's mother is its ultimate, inviolable haven. Once they entered their music, they remained effortlessly true to it and to themselves, regardless of the audience's reaction. They took it for granted that everybody would find it as engrossing as they did themselves. Musicians like Amir Khan and Nikhil Bannerji did not even raise their eyes during a performance because they were so deeply involved with what they were doing and oblivious of everything else. They were sure that nothing significant could possibly exist beyond the frontiers of their world of music. It is in this sense that I call them innocent. There are several anecdotes that illustrate this quality which characterised a whole generation of musicians.

Once Ustad Hafiz Ali Khan found himself sitting next to the President of India after he had received a state award. The president politely asked him what in his opinion the government could do to help the cause of music. After thinking carefully for a few moments, he said what can roughly be translated as: 'Sir, Darbari is in a very bad condition It is a great raga. People are treating it very badly, specially the *gandhara* and *dhaivata*. This is a serious matter. Please do something about it.' The president was understandably flustered and is reported to have instructed an attending official to 'look into the matter'.

Then there is the well-known story of Ustad Bundu Khan who, on being told that his scheduled broadcast had been cancelled because Mr. Jinnah had arrived unexpectedly and had to be fitted in the same slot, is reported to have said, again roughly translated: 'I have played with every musician in the country, but I've never even heard of this singer. What note does he use as his *sa*?'

Another telling incident is about Krishna Rao Shankar Pandit who was the guest of honour at a glittering function in New Delhi. Rajiv Gandhi happened to drop in since the venue was the house of a family friend. Naturally the hostess first introduced the chief guest. The eighty-year-old maestro beamed graciously at the clean-faced youngster who had come up to meet him. When his hostess murmured that this was the prime minister, he smiled at him and said 'Oh, then you must be the biggest person in Radio!' This was the first and most important thing that came to his mind!

Mallikarjun Mansur, it is often told, courteously turned down an invitation to perform for the Festival of India in America because the concert schedules interfered with the timings of his daily practice and meditation.

These are attractive and loveable personalities. One can hardly imagine people of this ilk performing with a sheaf of air tickets in their breast pockets in readiness for the flights they have to catch for their other engagements, or imitating the mannerisms and dress styles of megastars of Western jazz and rock music, or working the public relations circuits armed with glossy brochures listing their achievements and the standing ovations they received in this or that foreign country. In the old days no printed bio-data was ever asked for or needed. All publicity was by word of mouth and the grapevine of the music community. The artists themselves were usually no party to any promotional exercise that involved them personally. The point here is not that they were better people; only that their music reflected their absolute faith in their own world and therefore carried an indescribable depth and conviction which is rarely heard today.

That world has started to break up. The over-confidence which comes with easy access has affected not only audiences but also the new generation of learners. They are a breed apart from the worshipful disciples whose legendary devotion to the master and his art used to be a favourite feature of many a myth in the music world. They are much more canny and have a far more acute awareness of themselves as individuals. Even if they are associated with a particular musical cuisine or gharana they feel free to graze where they will and pick up whatever suits their repertoire and temperament at a particular phase in their career. *Alap* in the Kirana style, *taan* in the Jaipur style, *bol baant* in the Agra mode and *akar* in the manner of singers of the Patiala gharana can and do appear simultaneously in the performances of many young celebrities in the making. The walls of the gharanas are crumbling and have lost the will to keep their specialities to themselves. The newly acquired license to cater for a variety of tastes gives performers a heady feeling of freedom and power. Nothing is wrong with this except that dishes are being served before the cuisine has attained perfection. And this *is* a pity, as it robs the future of the ripest and richest fruits of single-minded concentration. The intelligent, confident, mobile, vitamin-enriched and uncommitted pupil of today feels he can get results even by sitting at the feet of a tape recorder if a guru is problematic. In the present set-up of musical education, he does not have to hang on the lips of a guru who is not likely to be available at his convenience if he is available at all. The musical aspirant today feels much more in control of his destiny. His fresh young mind is influenced by the systematic approach of Western researchers who are trained to ask questions and examine everything under a microscope. Unlike his earlier counterpart, he too demands a reason for everything. Armed with his tape recorder and cassette collection, he is sure that he can imitate any aspect of any gharana he fancies because he can repeat a lesson at will, and as many times as necessary. He does not need to collect carefully, memorise and cherish every pearl that might drop from the lips of a guru as it might not come his way again. Disciples of earlier generations had to do this as a matter of course.

But it has to be admitted that despite the ouster of devotion as the supreme quality in serious musical aspiration, the results are less disappointing than one feared. Never before have there been so many new 'prodigies' in both the Hindustani and Carnatic classical traditions. This phenomenon has less to do with population growth in general than with the devising of new learning techniques combined with the much higher level of efficiency and competence among the young. The substitution of devotion by skill, application, and an attitude of 'If anyone can do it, I can too' has been effective in ways that could be very important to the future of music in our country. Most of the new stars, especially in the Carnatic system, are in their teens and early twenties. The 'young' discoveries who were hailed by the world of Hindustani music only fifteen years ago are already presenting their own disciples on the stage! In addition to the crucial tape recorder, there is a battery of dependable gadgets such as electronic tanpuras and *taal-malas* which seem to work like seven-league boots for the new celebrities in the matter of their regular practice. The gradual fading of the *guru-shishya parampara* does not seem to have blocked the phenomenal increase in the number of whiz kids in both classical traditions. Organisers and impresarios do not any longer have to worry about who to feature in concerts because the possibilities are inexhaustible and still exceed the opportunities.

In this sense too, there has been progress. Something has undoubtedly been gained. At the same time a sense of loss pervades the ears that were young in the 1950s. To them, the intensity and conviction, the directness and innocence of the musicians of the earlier part of this century still have an unsurpassable musical quality which cannot be found in the most sophisticated recordings of today. As an old master put it, the clever new generation of musicians have eyes not only at the back of their heads but also in their armpits. According to him, too much seeing and too little intuition can rob the mind of its real musical potential.

Both the Hindustani and Carnatic systems of classical music demand a perseverance and concentration that is difficult to achieve in any circumstances. The existing distractions of modern life, for instance the persistent sounds of film music and commercial audio-cassettes offered almost round the clock by television and radio, make things even harder. The music that deluges us consists mainly of innovations devised by Indian composers on synthesisers and uses all the sounds of the world in an effort to present something that is both novel and instantly appealing. The music industry's frantic efforts to ensure that products are being manufactured in enough quantity to match the varied and ever growing demand has unleashed a new energy which speaks of the inexhaustible vigour and earthiness of our cultural roots even though all the efforts at composition may not qualify as great music. Nonetheless, I would say that of every five hundred unremarkable pieces which are likely to be self-conscious and imitative exercises in musical packaging, there is usually at least one which compels attention because it has been ignited by a genuinely creative imagination.

A desirable fall-out of this churning and exploring has been that musically the North and the South have come closer today than they have been for a long time. The new Indian pop and Hindi film music have performed the signal service of providing a common meeting ground for music directors from both systems. In fact the conservative South has been more enterprising than the North in this respect because the first real fusion trends were the contribution of music directors of Tamil films. It is now commonplace to hear *sargams* and *taalas* of the Carnatic system embroidering Hindustani raga-based pieces. The accompanying music of Bharatanatyam and Kathak often merge in depicting modern themes. Vocalists, instrumentalists and percussionists from both systems frequently appear together on stage in various permutations and combinations which do not fail to thrill the public. New music makers from the South are bestsellers in the North and singers from the South want to master thumri and ghazal. This was unthinkable even fifteen years ago when the two systems were disapproving and wary of each other even though they were tacitly agreed on the traditional promises of classical music—inner joy and the enrichment of the spirit.

Today, the term 'spirit' carries a different meaning altogether, something more akin to enthusiasm and optimism than anything to do with spirituality. People generally prefer to be teased and prodded rather than soothed and elated. This is what the new music maker caters for. At the centre of his tireless experimentation is a preoccupation with creating new sounds rather than with creating music. Indian folk and tribal music and elements of raga still provide the skeleton of most popular offerings, but the flesh defies identification. One can hear African and South American rhythms, melodies from the Middle East, Western-style delivery of pop songs, the sounds of Western jazz and much else in the music being produced in India today. This in itself is no disaster because Indian music has always absorbed influences from outside and integrated them into the mainstream. But the thread of continuity has always been there like a reassuring heartbeat. This sound is becoming fainter and sometimes cannot be heard at all.

Indian music cannot afford to sever *all* connection with its inherent values of purity and restraint. To the extent that these are diminished, the intrinsic quality of the music, however serviceable it may prove to be socially, suffers. At the same time music has to be the genuine product of an age. It must draw life and sustenance from its environment if it is not to degenerate into a museum piece. And herein lies the dilemma. There is no question that the musical forms and values associated with all traditional Indian music are in a state of flux. There is also no question that this is not the first time in history that this has happened. Change is always painful for the die-hards but experience tells us that it does not necessarily imply a negative development. When the khayal first established itself alongside the ancient dhrupad form around the fifteenth century it was considered an unworthy upstart and frowned upon by purists in much the same manner as music lovers who were young in the fifties view the innovations in Indian film and pop music today. Yet one has to admit that this unworthy upstart evolved into a rich and highly aesthetic form which is universally hailed as the finest flowering of the Hindustani raga system. It is relevant to remember that the khayal in its turn meted out to thumri and dadra the same treatment it had received itself at the hands of the dhrupad. Taking a lesson from this example in recent history, we must reserve judgement on the trends that are overtaking music in India today. It is perfectly possible that a new music which will be 'truer' to the times is in the making even as we speak. What seems sometimes to be an assault on ancient musical ears might well be the birth pangs of a new musical vision. The example of the khayal—there are many more—should caution us against instant assessment. The new pop music, whatever else it may lack, certainly is not feeble. On the contrary, it is almost always characterised by vigour, energy and an intense desire to communicate. Admittedly these are not enough to qualify sound as music but there is a fair chance that these could turn out to be positive attributes.

If music concerts are designed for two thousand rather than two hundred people, as indeed they should be, the intimacy of the baithak has obviously to be sacrificed. The change in the physical scene however presents some unforeseen difficulties which are not physical but have to do with the nature of the music that is being produced and presented. First, the ambience of the large auditorium is radically different from anything the musician's training and discipline have prepared him for. He can no longer find the same kind of inspiration from his distant audience as his guru probably could in old-style recitals by simply looking into the eyes of a listener and expressing what was in his heart. I remember a recent concert of Ustad Bismillah Khan in a large hall where he stopped midway and demanded that all the lights be turned on so that at least he could see who he was playing for. He said he wanted to let his shehnai address them directly. Needless to say, there was an immediate thaw in the atmosphere and the music he played after this spiralled to new heights. There are numerous examples where the presence or absence of rapport has made all the difference to the quality of the music at a performance. But the realities of the situation today cannot always accommodate this intrinsic requirement of our music.

Another intrinsic requirement is spontaneity. This too is less and less in evidence because of time constraints which foster an element of premeditation alien to the nature of Indian music. Some artists go so far as to work out exactly what they will do at a played concert, down to the last detail of rhythmic climaxes, fast runs, and other gems in their repertoire which are guaranteed to dazzle their listener. This road is yet another departure from the trodden path of genuine improvisation. In my view it is a threat to quality because the genius of Indian music does not lie in this direction but in the opposite one. The nature of Indian music is such that if it is pre-set, however roughly, in the manner of Western classical music, it can lose much of its power to infect and persuade, even though it still might fall pleasantly and tunefully on the ear. In this situation the musician has little chance of being able to *share* his spiritual striving with his listener. And this sharing is what our music is really all about. Everyone agrees with this—including the worst defaulters. Whether or not conditions permit intimate rapport and spontaneity, every performer on stage, radio and television compulsively simulates these characteristics, thereby paying unconscious tribute to these values in our traditional music. Ironically, even the most self-centred audiences are only impressed by the musician who ignores and disregards them because he is completely immersed in his own art.

Even though traditional practitioners try to accommodate their new audiences out of sheer self interest, they find it almost impossible to keep pace with modern electronics. The following advertisement I came across recently in a popular magazine is dramatic evidence of the explosion that has taken place:

Have you nurtured an unfulfilled desire to become a music director? Now here's your chance. The Miracle Piano Teaching System plugs into a Nintendo games machine or on IBM compatible computer and then works as a keyboard synthesizer. It has over 100 'voices' and has a full musical instrument digital interface (MIDI) compatibility so that it can be hooked on to other synthesizers.

The Miracle can also be a fun way to learn and to give lessons.

The second musical marvel is the Yamaha QY10. Smaller than a video cassette, the QY10 is a miniaturised MIDI sequencer. This means it scores MIDI notes and enables you to edit them, allowing you to work on eight compositions at a time. It has 76 pre-set accompaniments and drum patterns. So if music is the essence of life, here's your chance to play on.

The easy and informal language of the insertion suggests that the young music buff at whom it is aimed is not unfamiliar with the possibilities he is being invited to try out. On the other hand, his counterpart in the older generation is not likely to have the least idea what is being talked about. Never have things moved so far so fast. Along with physical and technological changes, the attitudes and awareness of society in general have also undergone a metamorphosis. A prominent signboard I saw on the façade of a small three-room flat at a street corner the other day announcing lessons in 'Western Dance, Guitar, Sitar, Cassio, Kathak, Painting and Folk' is a symptom of this metamorphosis. Such ambitious and confident enterprises are mushrooming all over the big cities. Among other things this tells us that culture has now become big business and that marketing might be a more important component of this business than art. Since this in turn depends on the number of consumers that can be drawn in, the emphasis has increasingly to be on what everybody understands, recognises, expects and wants. It follows that the lowest common denominator which satisfies the innumerable layers of the new urban and rural clientele will have to determine the nature of the product that is offered. This will automatically eliminate most of the subtleties and refinements.

Another area of danger is the growing tendency to concentrate on the physical aspects of sound rather than its meaning. It is an inalienable characteristic of Indian music that the intention of the performer takes precedence over the physical attractiveness of the sound. This is why some of the most sought-after musicians have been people in their seventies. This is also why disturbances such as clearing the throat or pauses for re-tuning in the middle of a traditional concert do not detract from the value of the music. So basic is this principle that even the uninitiated Indian ear is conditioned to it. A departure from these priorities could cut off a vital source of life.

But there are some hopeful signs. Regardless of their quality, the music videos that are flooding the market all aspire, perhaps unconsciously, to satisfy another central principle of raga, namely the gradual accumulation of musical meaning around a nucleus so as to suffuse the listener. The insistent refrains, the repetitive motif, the pounding rhythms of the videos aim at stimulating the senses into a heightened state of being, much in the same way as happens in keertan, qawwali, bhajan and even khayal. At the same time the presentation tends to be theatrical, aggressive and garish in a manner inimical to the nature of Indian music—as earlier generations understood it.

We are in the centre of a musical transition in which grace and romanticism, purity and restraint, depth and serenity, which still seem to us the most attractive attributes of Indian classical music, are receding. But music is not. Our lives are more full of sound than ever before. But it will be many years before we can clearly hear what it is saying to us.

AFTERWORD

Two Obituaries of Sheila Dhar

DILEEP PADGAONKAR: 'SHEILA'S SPELL'*

A marvellous singer and a spinner of fabulous yarns passed away in Delhi this week. Those who were privileged to hear Sheila Dhar's *gayaki* and listen to her ancedotes about musicians, bureaucrats, academics and even small fry will remain grateful to her for the joy she gave them in abundance. To be in her company was to enter a world where song and laughter, elegant living and learning borne lightly, reigned supreme.

I got to know the Dhars when I moved to Delhi in the early 1970s. Professor P.N. Dhar then served as one of Prime Minister Indira Gandhi's closest advisors. He and Sheila were possibly the most attractive 'power couple' in the Capital during that period. They were an unlikely pair. He tended to be taciturn; she was gregarious. His manner was subdued, somewhat cold and courtly. She was expansive, forceful, entirely natural. His smile was pinched. Her laughter was full, free, *bindaas*. The different temperaments were easily explained. He was a Kashmiri Brahmin. She was a Mathur Kayastha from Delhi. He epitomised the 'life examined' and she the graces of a refined lifestyle. But both shared much in common too. They were fiercely attached to their integrity. This is no easy task in the best of times. But in those years,

*First published in *The Sunday Times of India*, New Delhi, 29 July 2001.

when sycophants ran amok, safeguarding one's integrity required uncommon courage. The Dhars did not hesitate to mix with friends who Indira Gandhi had blacklisted. They expressed their opinions with a candour that seldom failed to surprise us. To be candid during the Emergency, especially when one was placed in a vantage position in the power structure, was to expose oneself to the risks of humiliation, harassment and worse. They chose to remain true to themselves: liberal, sensible, balanced and outspoken.

Six years ago, Sheila published a book of her reminiscences which generated enthusiastic reviews. She wrote with verve and humour about the lifestyle of the Mathur Kayasthas in the Delhi on the 1940s and '50s, gave scintillating accounts of her exposure to the great musicians of the time—Bade Ghulam Ali Khan, Kesarbai Kerkar, Pram Nath, Begum Akhtar, Siddheshwari Devi among others—and offered delightful vignettes about life in the bureaucracy. I have not read a more pleasant book about musicians before the appearance of this one, or since.

She was sixteen when her father asked her to receive Bade Ghulam Ali Khan at the station, escort him and his accompanists to the house of the host and fetch them to the concert hall after they had refreshed themselves and had their dinner. The hosts happened to be vegetarians. The maestro could not stomach the sight of this unfamiliar food. He exploded: 'Do you think I can sing the way I do if I have to feed on grasses swimming in fluids of various kinds? Every note I sing has the aroma of *kebabs*.' Sheila then describes how everyone ran helter-skelter to prepare a meal consisting of a rich chicken curry. That day, she writes, 'hearing him was pure and instant intoxication.'

In these memoirs Sheila displays a huge talent to write about music without the least jargon or pretentiousness. From Pran Nath, for example, she learnt to think about ragas in terms of colours. 'It was natural for him to dive into the dark depths of early morning ragas like Lalit and Bhairava, where there was no sun. Sometimes we would hear the greys and dusky ochres of twilight ragas like Puriya and Marwa, the midnight blue of magical and mysterious ragas like Malkauns and even the restrained gold of the majestic and courtly Darbari.'

Another gift of Sheila's that stood out in the memoirs was her ability to speak about the fads, eccentricities and weaknesses of people without a trace of malice. I have read with delight over and over again her chapters on the rivalry between Begum Akhtar and Siddheshwari Devi. Much the same thing can be said about the pages she devotes to her boss in the Publications Division, Mohan Rao, who imposes his overbearing hospitality on Richard Attenborough with a South Indian vegetarian meal. The guest looked visibly uneasy and at one point could not help saying: 'How do you chaps manage to eat this stuff? To me it tastes like stewed armpits!'

Such was Sheila Dhar: a singularly talented woman who sailed through life on the strength of her songs and stories and an inexhaustible capacity to laugh and make others join in her laughter.

RUKUN ADVANI: 'PUNGENT MELODY: THE LIFE OF SHEILA DHAR'*

Sheila Dhar, the singer of Hindustani classical music who died at the age of seventy-two last month, will not be remembered as much for her singing as for what she wrote about the practitioners and practice of singing. She would have sounded surprised if told—and her passion for music would never have let her admit it—that her real forté was the written word, and that she was actually among the most classically accomplished writers of evocative English prose any Indian has written over the past fifty years. Though she wrote three books—the first one, *Children's History of India*, appeared in 1961 and the second, *This India* (with a foreword by Indira Gandhi), in 1973— the clearest evidence of her art is her third book, *Here's Someone I'd Like You to Meet* (1995). The extended clumsiness of the title, rather like the

*First published in *The Hindu*, Sunday Magazine Section, 26 August 2001.

unwieldiness of her own physique in old age, is completely at odds with the idiosyncratic and idiomatic charm, the vivacity and infectious liveliness that lay inside her capacious body and which has been remarked upon by all who have read this gem of a slim-little-book.

She was no child Mozart and her early career, though academically first class, did not promise such unusual writerly blossom in late middle age. She was briefly forced by her family to study medicine—'they just needed a doctor at large', she once quipped, 'and since I was already large all that remained was the doctor bit.' But medicine was not music to her ears and she walked out of Lady Hardinge Medical College within a year in disgust: the smell of the laboratories could not be disguised even with furtive cigarettes. Dropping a year, she switched to Hindu College and topped her Delhi University English Honours batch in 1950 with a record-breaking score, married Professor P.N. Dhar the following year, accompanied him on his stint at Harvard, was awarded a *Summa Cum Laude* for her M.A. by Boston University, taught Literature for a short while at Miranda House, and then joined the government's Publications Division where, she said, 'I was immediately given the thrilling task of editing books with titles like "Home Care of the TB Patients" and "Sustainable Development of the Timber Forests in Andamans and Nicobars".' Every time she said something self-deprecating like this her eyes would narrow with suppressed merriment and she would explode into laughs. Every time she said anything at all, you could sense an impatient queue of wicked grins inside her, just waiting to get out and rearrange her face into a hawkish guffaw. She was a ready-made iconoclast, a natural mimic, and the cleverest raconteur of hilarious stories from real life about real people that it is possible to imagine. It was difficult to sit in her company and not be rolling about the floor.

No description of what it felt like to be within her ambience really makes much sense in words because she possessed the kind of intellectual liveliness and emotional warmth that has to be experienced to be believed. Her normal way of talking, of just being ordinarily herself, suggested she was three times as alive as anyone else. It seemed to account for her size. Some of her friends, having sensed this was an extraordinary being who did not so much radiate charisma as encompass it and transcend it at the same time, tried to get her on film, but she was very much a part of the oral tradition, she didn't like the sound and smell of celluloid, she become uncharacteristically morose facing the camera, the film was a flop, and so it is doubly unfortunate that words fail in trying to recapture her.

The nearest thing anyone can now do to get some sense of her living personality, even better than listening to cassettes of her singing, is to read her incredibly sparky prose, in which she manages to mould impeccable, grammatical and refined English sentences to serve the needs of quintessentially *desi* situations, dialogue and characters, a feat which defies all but the very best who strive to translate hybrid and locally specific Indian experience into English. She does this even better than Arundhati Roy, whose book she greatly admired for this specific reason. 'That girl', she once memorably said, 'has made English sentences perform Bharata-Natyam on a tightrope of coconut fibres.'

Her central interest in all she wrote was to communicate what it really felt like to be alive in the presence of certain people who had captivated her, or taught her to think or sing, or to look at the world from a slightly different angle. In *Here's Someone* these are usually Hindustani musicians and singers, but in *Children's History of India* they are historical personages. In the latter book, she said, the idea was to write history without dates, a notion that standard historians thought senseless but which was a great hit with children. She argued that children are definably children only so long as they want to know just what happened next, not when it happened. The moment they ask 'when did Aurangzeb become emperor?' is when 'they have grown up, and then they should stop reading my book.' Her argument was that children should remain 'prehistoric' and 'timeless', they would be stuffed with dates and facts in any case when they grew up. Nehru, a historian himself, thought this an odd but wonderfully eccentric assumption on which to base a history book for children. He wrote a preface for it, the book became a huge bestseller and went into sixteen impressions (it remains in print to this day), and it was translated into all fourteen Indian languages in the 1960s. Sheila Dhar returned Nehru's favour by editing a very large number of his speeches for him. Later, persuaded by Pupul Jayakar during the first Festival of India, she was instrumental in putting together a Leavisite LP titled 'The Great Tradition: Masters of Indian Music'. Her argument here was that a distinction needs to be made between 'musicians' and 'performers'. The former were those who forged the language of music. These included Zohra Bai, Abdul Karim Khan, Fayyaz Khan, Kesar Bai, Mallikarjun, Amir Khan, Gangubai, and Bade Ghulam Ali Khan. The latter were virtuoso artists whose accomplishment, no less considerable on a different stage, is mistakenly demeaned by comparison. Among these superlative performers she listed Bhimsen Joshi, Begum Akhtar and Rashid Khan. Kishori Amonkar, she felt, belonged to both categories, 'depending on her mood on a particular day'. Today, Sheila Dhar's canon of music is available in the shape of the 'Music Today' cassettes and CD's, for it was she who advised the producers and selected the performers.

Sheila Dhar's irreverent and balloon-pricking temperament had to be curbed when she started training to be a singer of Hindustani classical music, for the culture of this musical tradition is feudal and devotional, requiring something between deep respect and unquestioning worship of the *ustaad* by the *shagird*. Her years of rigour were, all the same, interspersed with long intervals of relaxed conversation with and observation of the likes of Begum Akhtar, Bade Ghulam Ali Khan, Siddheshwari, and Bhimsen Joshi, all of whom feature within her chapters on musicians in *Here's Someone*. She remarks on the sometimes insufferable narcissism of Indian musicians, pointing out that this is almost a religious tenet within their culture, but also one of its unlovelier aspects. The book mixes iconoclastic observation with an insider's casually deep knowledge of music-making in north India.

There is nothing quite like it. It is intensely alive, each chapter a riveting

AFTERWORD

story, each situation full of the most endearingly peculiar people, the whole book a memorable and treasured possession that enriches one's inner life incalculably and therefore something one keeps wanting to re-read again and again. There is also within it Sheila Dhar's personal trademark of acute perceptiveness about foibles of character, nuances of situational atmosphere, and subtleties of musical culture on the one hand, and an ability to kill us laughing at all of it on the other. Whereas the standard vocabulary of music criticism is completely technical at one end and effusively emotional at the other, hers does a better job than anyone else's in communicating something of the experience of Hindustani music to a lay listener. Using culinary metaphors which convey the 'taste' and 'fragrance' of specific melodies, she brings the tongue and the nose to bear upon the ear and does not hesitate to use the oddest analogies and examples if she believes they serve her literary and analytic purpose. 'My musical utterance inalienably carries within it the flavour of everything that has ever happened to me and of all the emotional landscapes I have traversed', she writes; actually, this is a description of her prose as well. The book also contains the most sociologically sharp evocation of a Kayastha household in pre-independence Old Delhi, a piece of informal literary anthropology which, for those to whom generic boundaries seem irrelevant, ranks with Malgudi and *The Remembered Village*. All this makes her book both an oddity and a masterpiece, though this is by no means the universal opinion on the book: many musicians and music critics who, unlike Sheila Dhar, cannot see that music can simultaneously be worshipped and its makers laughed at, have found her nonconformism unsettling. These are the people she always secretly wished to unsettle.

For she was an Epicurean in the classical mould: she had substituted the ridiculous idea of worshipping unseen gods with a passionate seeking out and sharing of friendship, music, and divine food, much of it cooked by herself. This was her notion of *advaita*. At the time of her death, Sheila Dhar was putting together a small collection of her essays. It will appear shortly, bearing a title which combines the two passions of her life: it is called *The Cooking of Music and Other Essays*. Madhur Jaffrey, one of her distant nieces, acknowledges several of her recipes as having been derived from 'Sheila'. Few know that this Sheila was Sheila Dhar.